Jo Wiltshire

The
Potty Training
Bible

This edition first published in Great Britain 2010 by
Crimson Publishing, a division of Crimson Business Ltd
Westminster House
Kew Road
Richmond
Surrey
TW9 2ND

A catalogue record for this book is available from the British
Library.

ISBN 978 1 90541 064 4

Printed and bound by Lego Print SpA, Trento

Acknowledgements

As usual, I must say a huge thank you to all the parents who have shared their tips and experiences with me, and been fantastically honest, entertaining and downright clever. My 'potty training families' were: Jane, Ant and Lola; Nikki, Gary and George; Gill, Alex, Stanley and Poppy; Sharon, Mark, Callum, Vincent and Lauren; Anton, Dougal, Jake, Eleanor, Buzz, Lara and Bibi; Sandra, Graham, Ben and Toby; Julie, Spencer, Emma and Josh; Mary-anne, Nigel, Kitty and Finn; Annie, Andrew, Tom and Olivia; Emma, Arif, Aisha, Anisa and Omar; Barbara, Mark, Kate and Victoria; Clare, Dave, Emma, Oliver, Evie and Hannah; Victoria, Justin and Elliott; Tania, Tom, Rebecca, Ashley and Vincent; Karen, Darren, Ellie and Pippa; Jill, David and Jessica; Jen, Dan, Lucas and Edmund; Emma, James and Cara; Jenny, Matt, Luke and Perry; Liat and Luca; Janet, Paul, Sarah, Mark, Jamie, Debbie and David; Kerry, Jon and Mason; Maxine, Dave, Marnie and Freddy; Gemma, Richard, Sara and Phoebe; Jo, Phil, Archie and Charlotte; Kate, Andy, Joe and Eddie.

Thank you too to June Rogers MBE, who was wonderfully enthusiastic about contributing to this book, and whose expert opinion is invaluable and much appreciated.

Thank you to Beth at White Ladder, for her spot-on advice. Thank you to Olivia, who helped me find some great willing contributors. And thank you to all at St Andrew's School, Much Hadham – especially Evie's friends' parents, whose children are owed a lot of play dates at our house!

I must also thank my wonderful family, including my mother Annie, and Colin, who give up so much time for us and who often held the fort while I wrote; my mother-in-law Christine, along with Maxine, Dave, Marnie, Freddy and Estelle, who helped entertain my babies on Saturdays when the deadline was looming; my father Tony, sister Lindsey, brother Jeff; and of course Lily the whippet, who dragged me out of the house to chase balls around the sheep field when writer's block set in.

Thank you to my Godmother Gloria, who is, and always will be, an inspiration.

A big thank you too to 'Nik-Nik', who keeps me laughing and looks after my boy, who loves her.

And most of all, thank you to my husband Lewis, who puts his family above everything and keeps us all close; and to my gorgeous children Evie and Charlie, who are everything in the world.

Thank you, too, for reading *The Potty Training Bible* – I wish you a very happy, nappy-free future. Good luck!

You can contact Jo at her website: www.jowiltshire.com.

Contents

Foreword

66 I'm impervious to poo, snot, urine, vomit. You can't get me. You cannot break me down.

Brad Pitt

99

I am just about to start potty training with my second child, Charlie. He is two years and nearly two months old.

There. After just one sentence of this book, most readers will already have made a judgement. Nearly two-and-a-quarter? 'About right', some will think. 'Why hurry? Let him do it when he's ready', others might wonder. 'Good grief, that child is practically in senior school – why didn't she have him on the pot a good year ago?' others might say.

And that is the issue with potty training. There is no manual that comes attached to your baby's left foot with a plastic tag, informing you exactly when this manufacturer's model is programmed to pee to order and when you should commence Operation Nappy Off.

Instead, parents face what seems to have become the standard mode of dispensing advice for the modern parent: a host of rather strident 'expert' voices promoting one method as a kind of mystical 'Potty Training Grail'. Add to this a barrage of accusing news stories, suggesting that whichever way you choose is intrinsically selfish and will damage your baby in ways untold. Oh, plus a good few all-too-readily aired personal opinions from your nearest and dearest.

The Potty Training Bible will be your breath of fresh air, in this rather pungent potty training environment. It will not preach. It will not tell you the way you are considering is wrong. It will not tell you there is only one way. And it will not assume that you and your baby have a textbook life into which any approach can be shoehorned rigidly and with no deviations.

This book is a practical, useful guide to a *range* of approaches to potty and toilet training, which doesn't promote one particular method with bias. It acknowledges different family requirements and different baby personalities, and will help you find the best solution tailored to *your* baby.

- Want to fit your potty training into one short, sharp but effective burst?

- Got an urgent deadline for dryness, or need to do the whole thing in one school holiday?

- Got another sibling on the way, and want to try potty training at an early age?

- Following a routine with your baby, and need to know how potty training can fit in with that?

- Can't stand the prospect of fights and tears, and believe there must be a calm, stress-free method to follow?

This book has all the answers – with expert opinion and top tips from parents who've tried each method.

Potty training often plunges families into trauma. Unlike those other 'big issues' of sleeping and eating, this is not something that has been a 'constant' from day one; part of everyday life. Instead, it's something which raises its head just when parents feel like the chaos of those early baby days is waning, and they are finally getting their lives back on track – until suddenly family life is dominated by a small plastic bowl and whether or not there is anything in it.

In this book you don't get a list of dos and don'ts. You get the information and advice you need to help you decide what *you* want. How *you* want to do it. And then *we* tell you *how*.

If you want to ditch the nappies *your* way, read *The Potty Training Bible*. Dryness awaits! Admittedly after a few, or even a lot, of puddles, but it's there. Hang on to that thought, and let's get started. And remember, when it's done, it's done forever!

Introduction

66 A child can only go so far in life without potty training. It is not mere coincidence that six of the last seven presidents were potty trained, not to mention nearly half of the nation's state legislators.

Dave Barry, American satirist 99

WHICH POTTY TRAINING APPROACH WILL SUIT YOU?

Haven't we all had it up to here with being told what to do? There are an awful lot of people out there who have very definite opinions about childcare and parenting issues. Authors, government officials, healthcare professionals, journalists, celebrities ... And yes, you might point out that I am one of those. But what I want to do is help you make your own mind up.

Now, many parenting guides are very informative and a huge lifeline for parents. The fact that parents these days have a sea of information about every aspect of childrearing at their fingertips, instead of being limited to what their own parents did, has to be a good thing. At least we can make informed choices.

But that's the thing. Where has the freedom to choose in peace gone? What about parents being credited with the intelligence to choose what's right for their family – and then being left to get on with it without constant superior heckling from the outside world?

When the time comes for you to potty train your child, you've probably already waded through a whole lot of expert advice, timetables and heartache regarding other issues in your child's life, such as sleeping and eating. You are all 'baby-booked' out. You look around, and find that indeed, those same gurus that helped you through the early stages are still around to tell you all about the correct approach to potty training. You might find this a relief. You might want an alternative. But the thought of going it alone and just doing the whole thing by instinct is a scary one. What if you get it wrong?

At the time of writing, there was a news story in the press which declared that teachers were blaming parents 'too busy to potty train' for an increase in children wearing nappies to school (*Daily Mail*, 3 August 2009). There were a lot of emotive words in this article. Parents had 'failed to toilet train their children', it said, leading to 'appalled teachers' refusing to take pupils who were still in nappies or who wet or soiled themselves, of which there were rising numbers. There was talk of working mothers too stretched for time to undertake potty training; of less pressure to conform, leading to lax parenting; of disposable nappies (which remove the discomfort of a soiled nappy) adding to the delay. Above all, there was an air of deep disapproval about the whole thing. As a parent, I certainly felt that a stern glance was being shot in my direction, lest I fail to present my son Charlie correctly at pre-school next Easter with a firm control of his bladder and bowels.

So I thought a lot about parental choice. And of course, the various methods of potty and toilet training available to parents differ wildly. Most 'big names' in parenting have given advice on potty training, as you might expect. Probably, most of these methods work. Eventually. Stick at something long enough and with enough determination and gusto, and it usually does – especially with children, who thrive on repetition.

It basically boils down to what method fits best into your life, and what suits your child's personality.

Read on, and once you've chosen a method, enter into it with the spirit of a warrior heading into battle armed with carpet stain remover and nerves of steel, and you and your child will emerge victorious. And nappy-free.

HOW TO USE THIS BOOK

The Potty Training Bible aims to lay out your options for you in a clear and easy-to-follow way. It will tell you what kinds of babies and families the various approaches might suit, give you some advice from real parents, and inform you how you can follow them too.

Each chapter tackles one of the big potty and toilet training steps – from preparing to start right through to dry nights.

Within each chapter, these issues are discussed through four different approaches:

- Early Days
- Non-Stop Bot
- By The Clock
- Gently Does It

These are my terms – they broadly group the most common and most widely known methods into clear and easy approaches with their own distinctive timings, ethos and appeal. The four approaches are briefly discussed below.

EARLY DAYS

Methods which deliver a potty-trained child at an early age or very early age: **the old-fashioned approach**.

The Early Days approach is good for big families with babies on the way, and where young children need to be able to take responsibility for their own toilet needs at an early age. It might suit a child who can take instruction well, and who has a calm nature. It would need a high degree of parental time and involvement, and one-to-one attention. It might not suit those who can't or don't want to put in the hard work early on, or who believe that 'these things happen in their own good time'.

> 66 This method doesn't necessarily guarantee early potty training success, and is time consuming and needs a lot of commitment. 99

June Rogers, continence expert

> 66 We co-sleep with Lola, and it was just a natural progression to take a similar "natural" approach to her potty training. Yes, it's a lot of work, but it makes you feel so close to your baby. I can't imagine doing it any other way — she's now one and hardly ever has accidents. 99

Jane, mother of Lola, one

Sound good? Then you might like the methods of Laurie Boucke; Dr Linda Sonna; Christine Gross-Loh.

NON-STOP BOT

Methods which achieve dryness and cleanliness in a short time: **the hurried approach**.

The Non-Stop Bot approach is fantastic for parents who want to toilet train their child in a half-term holiday, or some time off work, or before an important date, or even in one day! It suits those who can't stand the thought of endless weeks of accidents on the carpet, or long drawn-out negotiations with an implacable toddler. It might not be so good for very young babies, or for those of a nervous disposition, or for those who cannot devote a dedicated block of time to the project. Again, success within a certain timeframe is not guaranteed.

66 This method has been shown to be less effective without professional supervision. It is also less effective if the child is a poor drinker and unable to increase fluid intake. 99

June Rogers, continence expert

66 We started with George a month after his second birthday, and he was dry during the day after a week. I was either just lucky, or I had a super-clever little boy! 99

Nikki, childminder and mother of George, six

Sound good? Then you might like the methods of Gina Ford; Dr Suzanne Riffel; Dr Phil; Narmin Parpia; Dr John Rosemond; Nathan Azrin & Richard Foxx.

BY THE CLOCK

Methods which fit in with routine-led parenting approaches, and defined sleep and nap times: **the structured approach**.

The By The Clock approach is a must for parents and babies who have been following routine-based parenting methods, and are wondering how such a massive lifestyle change will play havoc with their calm routine. It would probably suit children who are used to a predictable and definite routine, and families who thrive on structure. It might not suit 'go with the flow' families, those whose routines fluctuate, or parents who need spontaneity or feel restricted by a timetable.

66 This method requires a good " clear run " and parents need to be able to focus on the potty training and not much else.

June Rogers, continence expert 99

66 Stanley and Poppy are used to a lot of routine, so we went the same way for potty training. Stanley learned in about three or four weeks when he was about two-and-a-half, and Poppy is just about to start. It means you have to put other things to one side for a while, but it also means it's calm and consistent and doesn't drag on too long.

Alex, father of Stanley, four, and Poppy, two 99

Sound good? Then you might like the methods of Dr Suzanne Riffel; Gina Ford.

GENTLY DOES IT

Methods which aim for dryness and cleanliness without tears or stress: **the 'no-cry' approach**.

The Gently Does It approach is great for families who need to be flexible, and for parents who don't like the idea of forcing the issue and causing their child stress. It might suit those who have been used to the ideas of attachment parenting. It is not so good for families with urgent deadlines for dryness, or strict routines, or who feel uneasy with a free-and-easy parenting approach, or for families whose children need to start a pre-school or school with a no nappies policy.

> ❝ Delayed toilet training has been shown to increase the risk of the child developing bladder and bowel problems later on, including daytime wetting and stool withholding behaviour. ❞
>
> June Rogers, continence expert

> ❝ I am of the "wait until they are ready" school of thought. All three of mine only had a handful of accidents once we decided to take the plunge, but the boys were both just over three, which is quite late in some people's view. For me, it was better to be chilled about it than have several accidents a day for weeks, or even months if you try too early.
>
> Sharon, mother of Callum, six, Vincent, five, and Lauren, four ❞

Sound good? Then you might like the methods of Dr Benjamin Spock; T Berry Brazelton; Dr Sears; Tracey Hogg (The Baby Whisperer); Elizabeth Pantley; Dr Sears.

GIRLS AND BOYS

One of the complicating factors of potty and toilet training advice is that, unlike many other areas, it is directly affected by whether your child is a girl or a boy. Many other issues like sleeping or eating may be slightly affected by the mindsets and personalities of the different genders, but with potty training, you have to deal with obvious physical differences and requirements.

Therefore, each chapter of *The Potty Training Bible* contains special fact boxes called **Girls' Guide** and **Boys' Basics**. These indicate where particular methods might differ according to their use with girls or with boys, or give special tips to help a particular method work more easily with either gender.

REAL-LIFE AND EXPERT ADVICE

In addition to a discussion of the four approaches in each chapter, you will find tips, advice and accounts of experiences from parents who have tried it all.

Each chapter also contains tips and advice from June Rogers MBE, who is a paediatric nurse, continence advisor and potty training and bedwetting expert. June is Director of PromoCon based at the Disabled Living Centre in Manchester, and is seconded to Liverpool PTC as a Specialist Paediatric Continence Advisor.

NOTE FROM THE AUTHOR: You will notice that throughout the book the baby is referred to as 'they' and 'your child'. This is for consistency and ease of reading.

Pre-Potty Preparation

66 I was toilet trained at gunpoint.

Billy Braver, actor and comedian **99**

Potty training is not the kind of activity you would be advised to start on a whim. Choosing to whisk away those nappies for good one sunny Sunday afternoon, with not a stain remover or pre-bought pack of super-dooper pants with cartoons on in sight, is unlikely to be successful.

Whichever method you choose, you're more likely to generate results if you put a bit of thought into it first.

I like to think of potty training as something of a war. Not a war between you and your child – in fact, you are both on the same side. No – more of a battle in which fumbling little fingers, stubborn little minds, and small people with the attention span of Iggle Piggle but the ego of Genghis Khan, are overcome to achieve a glorious state of bottom bliss for all. If you go into this with a battle plan and some decent armoury, you will succeed.

CHOOSING YOUR MOMENT

When is the right time to start potty training? First of all, let's see what the general medical consensus is. These days, most experts suggest that the majority of children are physically ready to begin toilet training between 18 months and three years. However, this does not necessarily mean that they are psychologically or intellectually ready.

The culture and times we live in also have an effect. During the 1920s and 1930s, for instance, early training and rigid scheduling were in vogue, and a 1929 *Parents* magazine claimed that most healthy babies could be trained by eight weeks of age[1]. By the 1940s, paediatric experts such as Dr Benjamin Spock were telling parents to wait until they observed signs of developmental readiness in their children, and that rushing them with rigid training would lead to behavioural problems.

Generally, over time, parents have become less inclined to start potty training very early (at less than 18 months), and more inclined to try various methods rather than stick to one – namely, the simple removal of the nappy.

There are even differences in the average age of starting potty training for Caucasian and for Black parents, with Black parents tending to start earlier, according to healthcare experts[2].

So, it seems that the 'right time' for potty training is somewhat variable. What you need to do, then, is find the 'right time' for your child. That time might not be the first time you try – many parents and children don't get potty training right the first time around. Sometimes, simply waiting a while until your child is really ready for it can work wonders.

Key signs

There are certain signs you can keep an eye out for which will tell you when your child is ready to give up the nappies. If you are going for an Early Days approach, these will not apply so vigorously to you – you are accepting that you, rather than your child, will initially be taking responsibility for knowing when to 'go'. But for the other approaches, these are good to look out for.

Physical signs can include:

- You being able to tell when your child is about to urinate or have a bowel movement by their facial expressions, posture, or what they say

- Your child staying dry for at least two hours at a time

- Your child having regular bowel movements

Intellectual, cognitive and behavioural signs include:

- Your child being able to follow simple instructions

- An ability and willingness in your child to cooperate

- Their discomfort with a dirty nappy and desire to be changed

- Your child recognising when they have a full bladder or need to have a bowel movement

- Being able to tell you when they need to go

- Asking to use a potty or toilet, or to wear normal underwear

You also have to factor in when *you* are ready. What kind of a person are *you*? Do you want a short, sharp, gung-ho approach? Or could you cope with a long, hold-your-nerve, slowly-slowly approach?

Do you have external circumstances, dates or upcoming events which dictate the right time for you?

There are also certain times you should avoid at all costs, if you can:

- Shortly before a new baby is due

- When you are changing childminders or caregivers

- When your child will be undergoing any disruption or major change, such as starting playgroup or pre-school

- When your family is undergoing a period of change such as moving house or changing jobs

- When you are feeling particularly stressed or depressed

- When your child is under the weather
- When you know you don't have time to follow your chosen approach through

Having taken all this into account, you can now start deciding which potty training approach might be the right one for you and your child – and when might be a suitable time to start it.

You have the battle plan. Now it's time to stock up your arsenal of weapons!

EQUIPMENT

There is a basic set of equipment which is useful no matter what approach you decide on:

- **Potties**. Rather obvious, unless you're going for the 'straight onto the toilet' approach. Buy a few – one for upstairs, one for downstairs, one for Granny's house, one for the car... wherever you think is appropriate and wherever your child spends a lot of time. Standard models are very cheap so it doesn't cost a lot to get more than one.

- **A 'booster seat' for your loo**. Good for those missing out the potty stage, but also a good idea even when you are still using nappies, to make the transition easier.

- **Toilet paper**. Consider the moist wipes marketed at children – yes, they're a little more expensive, but so much easier when teaching children to wipe mucky bottoms.

- **Carpet stain remover, in a spray bottle**. Test a small patch first – some bleach the colour out of carpets.

- **A protective sheet, or plastic 'mucky mat'**, or even just an old plastic-backed bath mat.

> **"** The baby, who has four elder siblings, wanted her own potty, not the nice expensive one the others had already used. We bought a pink princess one that took her about a week to get used to, but she cracked it very easily.
>
> Anton, mother of Jake, 10, Eleanor, eight, Buzz, seven, Lara, five, and Bibi, three **"**

Once you have your basics, you can fine tune your stash of equipment according to your chosen method.

EARLY DAYS

What is it?

The Early Days approach is often referred to as 'infant potty training', 'natural infant hygiene', 'elimination communication', 'potty whispering' or simply 'early potty training'. It takes in a range of start times, from the first months after birth to around the 18 months stage.

Have you ever listened to your mother or an older relative commenting that, 'in my day, we had children potty trained by the age of one'? This is how they did it – although while certain methods popular between 1920 and 1940 relied on rather harsh discipline and punishment, the modern-day equivalent avoids that, and instead preaches intuition and communication between baby and parent.

This approach also takes reference from the school of thought that mothers in days gone by had to manage without nappies, and that families in many other cultures either reject or don't have access to nappies these days either.

Well-known experts who advise on this approach include Dr Linda Sonna, Christine Gross-Loh and Laurie Boucke. It is seen as a rather gentle, child-led approach to potty training, which involves learning your child's elimination body language, timing, patterns and vocalisations.

This is not an approach for the faint-hearted or for those short of time. It involves close observation and constant presence.

When can I start it?

Proponents of the Early Days approach say that there is a 'window of learning' between the ages of birth and six months, although some children are receptive to this approach beyond this age, and it can be adapted for older children.

The average 'age of completion' – where your child rarely has accidents any more – is probably around two years, although babies can often achieve good control for many months before this. Control of poos tends to be achieved quite early in infancy, but control of wees takes longer.

What is certain is that this is not a quick method – it takes dedication, patience, perseverance and an ability to remain calm. It is a long-term commitment for parents with plenty of time.

The cues that you will need to be able to pick up on to know when you and your baby are ready for Early Days are:

- Vocalisation
- Fussing or crying before, during, or after pooing or weeing
- Grunting before pooing
- Making their own unique 'toilet noise'
- Body language
- Going still or quiet while pooing or weeing
- Passing gas before pooing
- Tensing up or stiffening
- Squirming or wriggling
- Grimacing
- Flushing in the face
- Staring into the distance
- Having a look of intense concentration
- Kicking vigorously
- Pulling in stomach and pushing
- Patting or touching crotch area

How can I prepare?

Extra pieces of equipment you might like to consider include:

- A 'pee pot' or 'potty bowl', which is essentially a small pot – smaller than a regular potty – which you can put under your baby while they are sitting on your lap
- A folding travel potty
- Extra-small 'real underwear'
- Training pants

- A notebook to use as a 'hits and misses' journal to aid recognition of your baby's cues

There are online specialist 'elimination communication' or EC shops where you can get equipment aimed at young babies.

Bear in mind

The trend these days in the West is for later potty training. You are bound to get sideways glances or even downright hostile reactions if you follow this approach - although it is a growing movement in the USA. You have to feel pretty sure about this to follow it through.

Also - remember that small babies wee about 20-25 times a day! Can you keep up with the pace?

> When I first told my husband Ant that I wanted to get rid of the nappies as early as possible, he was horrified — especially since Lola was sleeping in our bed! I think he had visions of lots of soggy, smelly nights. But we made sure we had a potty bowl and some bed pads, and actually, he quickly got on board with it, and when he helped her do her first wee in a pot he was dancing around the room like a lunatic telling her what a clever girl she was.
>
> Jane, mother of Lola, one.

NON-STOP BOT

What is it?

How fast do you want to go? A fortnight? One week? One day? This is the approach for you.

Yes, really, there are methods out there which assure you that it is perfectly possible to potty train a child in 24 hours.

There are several different well-known methods which aim to get things done and dusted in a minimal amount of time. Gina Ford's *Potty Training in One Week* is one. There is also the *Train in a Day Method*, which was first made popular back in the 1970s by the authors Azrin and Foxx. More recently, Dr Phil and Narmin Parpia have endorsed similar methods.

With the one-day approach, the idea is to go cold turkey with the nappies, announcing one morning to your child that they will no longer wear one. The following hours have a definite structure which provides intensive training and hopefully a nappy-free child by bedtime.

Also worth mentioning is the wonderfully titled (and obviously American) *Naked and $75 Method*, endorsed by Dr John Rosemond. It involves leaving the child naked (at least from the waist down) for three to seven days while they learn how to use the toilet. The nakedness helps the child become aware of their bodily functions. The parent demonstrates and explains initially, but then remains hands-off. The $75 is for the inevitable carpet cleaning bill!

All of these methods require a rather gritty and gung-ho mindset on the part of the parents, and a desire to put up with a short, rather hellish time in order to achieve quick results. This book will tell you how to achieve a generally quick success, taking in the best points of the methods mentioned above.

> ❝ We had a potty on hand at all times, and lots of nakedness (hers, not mine!). If she weed on the grass, it didn't matter. And if she used the potty, she got a small treat.
>
> Jill, mother of Jessica, eight. ❞

When can I start it?

Non-Stop-Botters should aim to start when their child is at the stage of recognising when they need to wee or poo, and may be telling you so. An ability to get to a toilet (including possibly climbing stairs), to sit unaided on a potty, and to pull down clothing is desirable. This is not a method for very young infants because it promotes a child's desire for independence and requires a little more maturity.

Most children will develop the bowel, and especially the bladder, control necessary for this approach anywhere from the age of 18 months to over two years. Before this, they are unlikely to be able to hold themselves for long enough.

Other signs to watch for are:

- A child's nappy being dry after a daytime nap, or it being longer than two hours since the last nappy change
- An ability to follow simple instructions and directions
- A willingness to remove clothing and pull down trousers
- A knowledge of their own body parts and associated names

- An ability to sit still and occupy themselves for five minutes or so – while reading a book, playing or watching television.

How can I prepare?

Extra equipment that will be useful:

- A wee-proof pad or cushion for the car. You can buy these, or make your own by covering a thin cushion with a plastic bag and then putting on a cushion cover.

- Plenty of big girl or big boy underwear ... at least a week's worth, and preferably ones with appealing pictures on the front.

- A star chart or 'treat box', or hand stamps for rewards.

- A booster step.

- Some loose clothing, such as tracksuit bottoms or elasticated trousers.

You don't need to go mad with the fancy potty designs or other equipment – the aim is that this is a quick method which will lead rapidly on to toilet use anyway, so there's no point spending too much money on something which will soon be relegated to the loft. Some experts advise buying just a couple of cheap potties in the same colour (so that your child won't declare that they *must* wee in the blue one that is two flights of stairs away and that the green one in front of them simply won't do).

Bear in mind

This is a fantastic approach for parents who want – or need – to help their child potty train in a short time. But you have to be able to give it a short but dedicated time slot. Think ahead – can you book a holiday from work, or do it in half-term, or ask relatives to help out with other children while you concentrate on this?

The more focused you, as parents, are on the Non-Stop Bot approach, the more likely it is to work in the desired timeframe. This is not for the faint-hearted parent.

“ I made sure we had a potty in the lounge. I let George run around in his pants but asked him every 15 minutes, ‘Do you need a wee?’ He obviously got so fed up with me asking, because on day two I only said, ‘George...’ and he said, ‘No Mummy! I don’t!’ Poor thing, with a crazy, nagging mother.

Nikki, childminder and mother of George, six **”**

BY THE CLOCK

What is it?

The By The Clock approach is a structured, practical approach, which is ideal for those who have previously used structured parenting techniques for sleeping. Again, Gina Ford is a good port of call for methods which fit into this, along with Dr Suzanne Riffel.

This approach calls for consistency and for gradually training a child to take responsibility for their own bodies. It is usually fairly quick, although not as quick as a day! It can, however, be used for a week-long potty training timeslot.

There are some variations on this theme. The American 'Timer Method', for instance, is a technique which again has the child out of nappies during training, but also involves the use of a timer, set for predetermined intervals. When the timer goes off, the child is brought to the potty for a potty session. If the child is successful, a reward is given. The length of time between timer bells is gradually increased as the child becomes more reliable.

All variations in this approach tend to rely heavily on frequent reminders and lots of positive reinforcement through praise, incentives and rewards.

When can I start it?

As with Non-Stop Bot, the best time to start this approach is when your child can recognise their own need to wee or poo, can manage simple instructions and simple clothing, can concentrate for short periods of time, and responds well to praise and incentives such as star charts and rewards.

If you have a child who is very resistant to taking instructions, or is unable to be diverted by a book or TV show for a few minutes, then it might be best to leave it for a couple of months.

Starting too early with this kind of approach usually leads to failure – better to be 'all systems go' with a child who is fully ready and able to take it on.

This method also relies fairly heavily on consistency and structure. Don't start it if you are going through a time of upheaval, or have an important event, visit or holiday on the cards which will disrupt your normal daily routine. Pick a time when you can stay at home a lot, and when the odd damp trouser leg won't be taken out of proportion.

How can I prepare?

If you like the sound of a timer-style approach, maybe invest in a cheap kitchen timer. If you simply want to go for structure, then you won't need much other than the staples mentioned on p19.

What you could do, though, is practise 'sitting still for five minutes' – but not on a potty. Use a cushion on the floor, and read a story together or watch one short children's programme, such as an episode of *Thomas the Tank Engine* or *Angelina Ballerina*. This will help when your child has to sit and wait for inspiration at potty time.

Bear in mind

This is not for 'go-with-the-flow' parents! You cannot start this approach on day one, then get a phone call from a friend on day two and decide to up roots and pop into town with your child for a quick coffee, only to be disappointed when you find a puddle on the coffee shop floor.

This approach takes a willingness to stick to a plan and to follow it through. Clock watching comes as part of the parcel.

66 I started with Ben just before his second birthday, when we had time to concentrate on it. He chose his own potty, which I think helped him to get involved in the whole process. His birthday is in June, so a good time to try as he could wander around the garden and house in a long t-shirt and not a lot else. I sat him on it every 20 minutes

or so. He was very happy with himself when he did his first wee and I turned into an insane woman clapping and cheering around the garden — not sure what the neighbours thought!'

Sandra, mother of Ben, 12, and Toby, six

GENTLY DOES IT

What is it?

The Gently Does It approach is basically a 'child-centred' toilet training approach. What this means is that it puts the child in charge of when, and how, to train.

This is an approach for older children. It involves letting the child remain in nappies the entire time that they are comfortable with it, and waiting until they decide on their own that it is time to get rid of them. This typically happens around the age of two-and-a-half or older.

This kind of approach is becoming increasingly popular in the Western world. In fact, more and more parents are waiting until they absolutely have to train a child in order for them to start pre-school or school – and indeed some are even waiting longer and sending their child to school while still in nappies. The increasing demands on working women are also believed to have led to this trend – there is never a large enough block of time to potty train a young child.

The advantage of a Gently Does It approach is that children who reach this age and who make a decision on their own to ditch nappies are typically very easy to train. They are more mature, more dextrous, and can be reasoned with more easily.

However, the flip side is that for some children the habit of using nappies, and the acceptance of having soiled themselves, is so ingrained that they don't have the incentive to change – and convincing them to use a potty or toilet is difficult. Some even fear doing a poo without the 'safety net' of a nappy in place.

Child-centred potty training was first introduced in the early 1960s, when cloth nappies were still used. Disposable nappies, which appeared in the UK around the 1980s, kept the feelings of wetness and discomfort away from the child, giving them even less incentive to become trained.

Proponents of the child-centred approach include Dr T. Berry Brazelton. It is also adopted by the American Academy of Pediatrics and is probably the most used method in the United States.

Other considerations are that while this approach doesn't require much participation or dedicated time on the part of the parent, it does take a longer time than some other methods – up to six months or longer sometimes.

For parents who like the idea of a child-friendly approach that puts an emphasis on calmness and gentle tactics, but who cannot face just waiting until the child actually takes the lead, there is the 'no-cry' approach of experts such as Elizabeth Pantley, whose methods tend to be suitable for a later age group (two-and-a-half to four) but are instigated by the parent.

When can I start it?

The Gently Does It approach involves taking a lead on timing from your child. Whether you are leaving the decision entirely up to them, or simply looking for the cues that they are absolutely ready and mature enough for the transition, you will still look to them for that golden moment. Either they will overtly tell you or show you, or you will see from their abilities, signals and readiness.

Don't stress if opting for this approach means that your child's peers are already displaying their streamlined, nappy-free silhouettes long before your child shows an interest. There are stages to potty training – those children may be reliable some of the time, or at day but not at night, or in a potty but not a toilet. It is impossible to compare children, whose developmental milestones and personalities can be very different.

Nearly all children get there in the end – by waiting for your child to take the lead, you are showing them that they can be responsible for themselves and that you trust them. When it does happen, this can be extremely affirming for the child, who feels a real sense of accomplishment.

66 Don't bow to peer pressure. Archie started quite late, and for ages he weed sitting down because he'd only seen how girls do it. He's only started standing up in the last seven months or so, and now enjoys aiming at the flowers or the car wheel! Charlotte did it before she was two, because she was more practical and had Archie to copy.

Jo, mother of Archie, seven, and Charlotte, five 99

How can I prepare?

Start to talk to your child about using the potty or loo, to see if they have a positive response to you. They may be ready, but it simply hadn't occurred to them to begin.

To encourage them, get a star chart – an older child responds well to these.

Other useful equipment will include:

- A booster step and child-sized seat if they are going to go straight to the toilet stage.
- A commode-style seat potty if they prefer to start with a potty – this will suit a larger, taller frame more than a small, traditional potty.
- Children's potty story books that they may be able to help you read to them – older toddlers enjoy the example of the pictures, and can engage with the characters.

If your child is about to start pre-school, you might also be offered a visit to see the classroom and meet the teachers. Ask if you can show your child the toilet area – these usually have scaled-down toilets and small sinks, and are quite appealing. They might also see children near their own age using them, and be inspired. When they finally come to pre-school and have to use them, the toilets will be less daunting.

❝ In preparation for this method I would recommend the child is taken out of a disposable nappy and put in either a washable nappy or washable 'pull up'. From my experience this approach works better for little girls – most

> little boys are quite happy to stay in a disposable nappy and often require a more structured approach.
>
> June Rogers, continence expert

"

Bear in mind

Late potty training can be something of an issue with pre-schools, clubs or schools. Some will not admit a child who is still in nappies. Find out what your intended pre-school's policy is so that you can work with it.

Also bear in mind that waiting until a child tells you that they are ready will involve a greater financial outlay if using disposable nappies. You will probably have to splash out less on carpet cleaner when they do try though – their consistency, reliability and indeed their aim will be better.

" We're definitely in the 'leave it till later' camp. With Joe, we tried when he was about two-and-a-half. My friends (who all had girls) had all successfully trained their offspring to be dry and clean by day and I was seriously feeling the pressure. It was summer, and we were envisaging Joe playing in a sun-drenched garden all day with any accidents al fresco! He just wasn't ready – loads of mopping and wiping and chucking away of pants ensued so we abandoned it. We tried again when he was three – again, no joy. Eventually, a couple of months later he was playing next door and saw their little boy using the loo. That was it. He came back and by the end of the week he'd sorted wees. Poos were sorted a little later. When he finally wanted to do it, it was fairly quick and effective.

Kate, mother of Joe, five, and Eddie, three **99**

Girls' Guide

- To do a wee or poo, a girl needs to relax her pelvic muscles. She will find it easier to do this if she can put her feet on the floor or on a booster step. Her feet should be flat and her knees not too scrunched up to her ears.

- Girls are often interested in baby dolls that can be fed water, and then do a wee in a potty. My daughter Evie found her one slightly alarming, but others girls I have known have loved sitting on their potty with a baby doll next to them on a baby potty.

Boys' Basics

- Some boys do not like the idea of standing up to wee; it is fine for him to sit down for this. But if he does want to try, provide a potty for him to stand in front of – it is much easier for younger boys than balancing precariously on a step in front of a toilet.

- You might also want to invest in something appropriate to put down the toilet bowl to encourage him to aim accurately when he does get big enough. Best tips include a ping pong ball, food colouring (it changes colour), confetti, a waterproof sticker, coloured ice cubes, or even a few Cheerios!

"Apart from Early Days, regardless of which method you choose to potty train your child, preparation will make your life a lot easier. We always recommend that once your child is able to stand, then all nappy changes should be carried out in the bathroom with your child standing up. This enables your child to take a more active part in the process – they can start to learn about pulling pants up and down, and bottom wiping, for example. If they have done a poo (and it's not too squashed in the nappy!) this can then be emptied into the toilet with the child waving it 'bye bye', then flushing it away and washing and drying their hands. "

June Rogers, continence expert

[1] Luxem, M, Christophersen, E, Behavioural toilet training in early childhood: research, practice, and implications. *Journal of Developmental and Behavioral Pediatrics* 1994; 15:370

[2] Horn, IB, Brenner, R, Rao, M, Chen, TL, Beliefs about the appropriate age for initiating toilet training: are there racial and socioeconomic differences? *Journal of Pediatrics* 2006; 149:165

Potty Power – How to Get Started

66 Politicians and nappies have one thing in common: they should both be changed regularly and for the same reason.

Anonymous
99

By now, you've hopefully decided on a battle plan – your chosen approach – and have a fully stocked arsenal of potty training weapons. All you need now is the will to get going – and a cooperative little soldier-in-arms!

But first, here's a quick look at some 'terminology'. By this, I mean the terms: potty training, toilet training and potty learning.

At the end of the day, all any parent wants is the 'end result' – a child who can take themselves off to the toilet without reminders, and keep themselves clean and hygienic in the process. So whatever term we use for the process by which they get there is not really that important. Some parents would prefer their child to start with a potty and then move on to using the toilet. Some would prefer to skip the potty stage. Some children will have a strong preference for one or the other, and sometimes the choice will be dictated by the child's age or ability.

As far as 'training' versus 'learning' is concerned, most parents agree that the process should be about a child *learning* to predict, control and manage going to the loo, with the help and encouragement of their parents. After all, the word *training* just brings to mind mice in cages ringing bells for food, or dogs on leads.

However, most of us are used to the conventional stock phrases 'potty training' and 'toilet training', and feel comfortable with these, and that is why they are used in this book. As for the actual advice given, much of it is applicable whether or not your child's bottom is hovering over a plastic potty or a toilet seat. You can adapt it. This chapter will concentrate on starting off on a potty, because many parents go down this route. The next chapter will deal with moving from potty to toilet, or going straight to using the toilet, in more detail.

TOILET TERMINOLOGY

While we're on the subject of naming things, we should also mention the terms you decide to use for body parts and bodily functions. This is really your family's own decision. It will depend on what you, your family and the people you spend the most time with say, and feel is acceptable.

In our house, we stick with 'poo' and 'wee' for bowel movements and urination. Some people use 'Number One' and 'Number Two'; some people opt for the American 'pee' and 'BM' (bowel movement). Some families even create their own terms which can be as imaginative as you like.

Throughout this book, we use the terms wee and poo to describe these bodily functions. While it might not be particularly refined, our main concern is giving you clear information, so please overlook our frank terminology!

You shouldn't feel embarrassed that you don't use 'grown-up' terms for these – even doctors, when talking to children, use 'poo' and 'wee'. But it is worth trying to teach your child that when out in public, you can use a 'catch-all' term such as 'needing the loo' or 'needing to go' rather than describing in graphic detail precisely which function is urgent! Likewise, try to find terms for body parts which are acceptable both at home and in a wider context, such as pre-school and eventually school.

Vocabulary for bottoms might include vagina, privates, front bottom, bits or even gina for girls; for boys it might include penis, willy or pee-pee. You might also need terms for passing gas – since it is often a sign that a child needs a poo – and these might be anything from passing wind to blowing off to plain farting. Our term is 'doing a pop-pop'!

In addition, try to start introducing other useful terms which will help your child understand the whole toilet process, such as:

- Wash
- Flush
- Pull down
- Pull up
- Wet
- Dry
- On
- Off
- Now
- Later
- Desperate!

These will help your child vocalise their actions and needs, which will help you and will also reinforce their learning.

So – everything is ready to go. In the first chapter we discussed *when* you might be ready to start. Now we will tackle *how*.

Firstly, grab your diary. Find a time when – realistically – you can expect to fit your chosen approach into your life.

Next, grab a pen and *ink it in*. Indelible ink. Mark it on a wall calendar, agree it with your partner, tell the grandparents, maybe even do a round-robin email to all who know you or your child. The more incentive you have to stick to a start date, the better.

Finally, grab a few good bottles of wine, or a stock of favourite films, or a box-set of *Friends*, or whatever you normally treat yourself to when you need to relax. Have them on stand-by, and promise yourself a tiny window of wind-down time – it could be an hour before you go to bed each night, or one evening a week – when you will recover from battle and recoup. If you know there is a tiny puddle-free patch of 'me time' in store, it's amazing how calmly you can mop up accidents and fish the sixth pair of clean pants out of the top drawer.

That done, you need to get going.

EARLY DAYS

Getting started

First off, you will need to get used to the idea that an Early Days approach is not a 'training' method as such.

At the very beginning, this approach is more a way of taking care of a baby's needs in preparation for their eventual ability to manage it themselves – a natural progression, rather like that from breastfeeding to eating independently. So from the start, there is nothing terribly complicated about getting going. Messy sometimes, maybe, but not complicated.

Assuming you have chosen your baby's normal intended place to 'go' – a potty, pee pot, bucket or the loo – you simply anticipate when your child needs to go from the list of 'cues' in Chapter One. Then at that moment, pick them up, hold them gently and securely over the desired receptacle, and make a watery sound such as 'ssss' or 'psss'. Even if you don't anticipate in time, and catch them in mid flow, still make the sound, which they will come to associate with the action.

43

If you are holding your child, they will be able to relax their muscles and release the wee – and they will associate both your 'ssss' sound and this position with relieving themselves. You should be holding your child with their back firmly against your chest or upper stomach, supporting under their thighs with your hands.

Bear in mind that most young babies need to relieve themselves around 20 minutes after eating, and upon first waking up after a sleep or nap.

The first time your baby actually produces a wee, you will experience a huge feeling of elation and your baby will pick up on this – offer lots of praise, and reinforce your 'ssss' sound.

You can move on to 'poop-poop' or making 'hmmm hmmm' sounds as soon as you like. Many parents recommend that, for bowel movements, the parent sits on the floor with knees bent and the child sits facing the parent, with their legs over the parent's legs, so that the parent has formed a kind of 'potty' seat for the child.

Getting it right

With the Early Days approach, it really is a case of 'repeat, repeat, repeat'. Every time you 'catch' a wee or poo, celebrate. If you 'miss' one, try to remain calm, and say something along the lines of, 'We missed a wee, we'll get the next one ...'

As you move from the first days of trying, remind yourself of the four important factors that will help you and your child work together to get it right:

- **Timing**. Newborns tend to urinate every 10–20 minutes. As they grow, the gaps get bigger. By six months, the gap between wees while awake may be up to an hour (babies, like adults, rarely urinate when sleeping deeply). Poos tend to be more individual to your baby – some do several a day and others go several days without one. Try to note down your baby's pattern.

- **Signals**. Some babies have very obvious signals, and others have subtle ones. These might be a certain facial expression, a certain cry, squirming, going very still, crankiness or fussing, stopping sucking while feeding, or passing gas.

- **Cueing**. This is *your* 'signal' – the sound you make while your baby wees or poos. It tells your baby when it is okay to 'go'. At first, your cue will happen *while* the baby is 'going', but later you can use it to indicate that she is in a safe place to 'go' and that she should do so. This is useful if you are in a friend's house or a public toilet or anywhere they are not familiar with, to let them know that this is an appropriate toilet place. Also note that older babies might like to learn a word rather than a 'toilet sound', and can even learn a discreet non-verbal signal.

- **Intuition**. You will be amazed that, as you and your child learn together, you will develop a kind of 'sixth sense' that they need to 'go'. Pair this with your cues and signals and knowledge of their timings, and trust yourself.

Extra tips for success

Remember that notebook or journal that was on your list of things to buy before you started? Now is the time to use it. Start making a note of every time your baby does a poo or wee. It doesn't need to be complicated or detailed – you could devise a code for quick reference, such as a tick for a 'catch' and a dash for a 'miss', with a 'w' or a 'p' next to these to indicate wee or poo. This will help you enormously in identifying your baby's timings, and also any 'weak times' when you consistently fail to anticipate your baby's need to 'go' – such as tea-time, or at the end of the day when you are both tired.

66 We started very early with Kitty and now with Finn. With Kitty, I was still working part-time so it was a bit of a nightmare and I couldn't have done it if my mother hadn't stepped in to babysit – I taught her all of Kitty's cue noises! With Finn, I'm now at home all the time so it's much easier, but we still make sure the grandparents know the cue noises and signs, because it's not always you who is on the scene when they need to go!

Mary-anne, mother of Kitty, three, and Finn, 11 months 99

NON-STOP BOT

Getting started

First of all, let's make it clear that whether you are aiming to 'train in one day' or 'train in a week' or any other variation that promises a rapid result, if you think you can simply wake up one morning, decide it's 'The Day' and launch into it with no prior preparation, you're mistaken. Most 'quick result' approaches actually rely on some detailed forethought and planning to achieve that impressive success.

Ways that you can build up to your actual 'this is it!' time to ensure that it stands a chance of working are:

- When you observe the signs in Chapter One that your child is psychologically and physiologically ready, put a potty upstairs in the bathroom and downstairs in a convenient spot. Let them touch it, sit on it. Explain to them what it is for.

- Let your child see you going to the loo. Wees will do if you cannot face a public demonstration of a bowel movement. Ask your partner to let themselves be observed as well.

- Don't just wait for them to walk in on you. Say, 'Ooh, Mummy/Daddy needs a wee. I'm going upstairs to the loo. Do you want to come?' They will learn that you are thinking about the need to 'go' before you actually do it.

- Talk them through what you are doing – 'Mummy's pulling down her trousers and knickers, Mummy's sitting down on the seat – do you want to sit on your potty? Mummy's wiping with the toilet paper, Mummy's flushing and then washing her hands ...'

- Create certain times when they are allowed to sit for a few minutes on their potty with no nappy on – a good time to start is at bath time while you are running the water, after breakfast and then after naps.

- Consider buying a doll that 'wees' water. Let your child play with it, sit it on a doll's potty or their own potty. Use role-play to explain what dolly needs to do.

Then – it's D-Day. On your chosen morning, you announce to your child that they will no longer wear nappies. Some parents like to make this an 'out of our hands' situation – they explain that the nappies have run out, that the shop hasn't got any, or that the nappy fairy has said it's time to let a smaller baby have the nappies now. However you play it, be firm but warm. This is exciting news – not the toll of doom.

Next, reinforce all the preparation you have been doing. Run through the 'procedure' – talk about where the potties are, how to get there, how to tell Mummy or Daddy. It is useful to talk to children about the 'feeling' they get in their bottoms or tummies when they need to 'go' – some children don't automatically recognise this signal, and therefore fail to anticipate the need in time. Telling them in words what this feels like often helps.

Once you have done this, you are well and truly in the thick of it. Try to remove treasured rugs or cushions. Put them in a pair of easily removed knickers or pants, and turn up the heating a little if it is winter.

At this point, opinion differs as to what your own involvement should be. Some methods advocate lots of positive reinforcement when the child is successful, and negative enforcement through certain 'toilet drills' when there is an accident. The positive could be a reward, a potty part or a superhero phone call. The negative enforcement drill is essentially a practice run-through of what should have happened.

Other methods prefer the parent to be studiously 'hands-off' at this stage. In particular, those that advocate your child being naked from the waist down tell you to leave the child to become aware of their bodily function (easy when it's running down their leg!) and learn to deal with it. The parent is there to help, but doesn't get actively involved in praising and reminding every few minutes.

Do what feels right. Don't act like a drill sergeant, but don't disappear off to the bottom of the garden and let them cope alone either. A lot of observation and a timely helping hand when needed is probably the right balance.

Getting it right

The point of a quick-fire potty training method is that the responsibility for toileting quickly passes from parent to child. Imagine you have paid for a day course at a cookery school. What will happen?

First, you will be dressed appropriately and shown the relevant equipment. Then you will watch a chef demonstrate a particular recipe or method of cooking. Then you will be shown your own ingredients and asked to repeat this yourself, with chef standing by in case of culinary disaster. But when you go home, chef doesn't come too. There comes a point when you will practise your newly learned skill at home, on your own. You might not get it perfect first time without their expert guidance, but with practice you will soon have it down pat.

This is what you are aiming for with a Non-Stop Bot approach. Within a very short time, your child will know what is expected of them. They will be familiar with the equipment, comfortable with the routine, and much of the time will be able to follow it, at first with your reassuring presence, and then on their own.

Of course, there will be accidents. No child can be 100% reliable after one day, or one week. But what has been learned in that time is the *routine*, the *desired behaviour*.

So if the odd accident happens, don't throw your hands up in despair, chuck the wet pants in the bath and throw a nappy back on your child. This will in one fell swoop undermine all the confidence in their own abilities that your child has worked so hard on. Stick with it, trust them, and gradually their body will catch up with what their mind has already taken on board.

Extra tips for success

Whether you are involving yourself overtly or trying to stay in the background, try to put aside distractions. Turn off your phone; don't arrange anything important; don't have friends round. Even though your child is in the spotlight, this is a joint effort and deserving of your full attention.

Also, try to arrange lots of things to keep your child busy that you can be involved with too – like a jigsaw, a game, drawing, or watching a video together. That way, you can be close to your child and observe them without them feeling like you are looming over them in an unnatural and off-putting fashion.

If you have had any success *at all* by the end of the day, celebrate it. Even if it is one tiny puddle in the potty. Don't refer to accidents, just praise successes. Your child needs to go to sleep basking in the glow of your approval, so that they wake up with the desire to give it another go, rather than feeling dispirited.

" A number of these methods also advocate giving the child extra drinks during the training which ensures regular trips are required to the potty! **"**

June Rogers, continence expert

> ❝ Buzz learned very quickly at two-and-a-half because he wanted to go on a camping trip with his Dad – and the only way Dad would take him was if he was out of nappies! He literally learned overnight – he never had an accident!
>
> Anton, mother of Jake, 10, Eleanor, eight, Buzz, seven, Lara, five, and Bibi, three ❞

BY THE CLOCK

Getting started

This approach relies just as much on timing and cues as does the Early Days approach. The difference is that your child is older, and has a more predictable and defined routine than a newborn or very small baby. Therefore, the responsibility for 'going' passes to them, rather than it being a team effort.

With a routine-based, structured potty training approach, organisation is key. So when you are ready to begin, spend a week or so plotting your child's normal weeing and pooing routine on a chart. During this time, you can follow the preparation advice for Non-Stop Botters – let your child get accustomed to their potty, observe you on the loo, and go through the desired routine with you.

Closely observe the times that your child tends to do a poo, the length of time between soggy nappies, and how these all fit in with their daily routine of eating, sleeping and playing.

The chances are that if you are attracted to a By The Clock approach, you may well have followed a routine-based approach to baby sleep from the early days. Your child, by now, is probably sleeping through the night in their own bedroom or nursery, can get themselves to sleep, and is accustomed to taking at least one nap a day in their own bed at a particular time.

The advantage of this is that your child has been set up from the very start of their life to take responsibility for their own needs in a secure environment without panicking. This will help a lot when they enter the realm of potty training. The trick, then, is to find a way to work in using a potty so that, for them, it is simply another small, unobtrusive element of their usual calm, predictable day.

A child who is used to a By The Clock approach to life is generally quite keen on the idea of independence. You can play on this by letting them get involved in the preparations for potty training. Take them to the shops and let them pick out their own underwear. For both girls and boys, there are some fantastic ones with characters on the front. Let them decide exactly where the potties in your house should go. Maybe even let them decide, with you, when the 'start date' should be. And then, on Day One, remind them that today is the day, and that they will start their new 'big girl/boy' routine.

Remember, you will have worked out in advance what time they are most likely to need to 'go'. This might be on waking, after breakfast, before nap, after nap, before lunch, after lunch etc. When it is time, simply say to your child, 'Potty time' and lead them gently to the potty. Then say, 'Let's sit down and wait for a while to see if anything's ready'.

Try to reinforce the idea that they will 'try' at certain times regardless – but that if they need to go in-between a regular visit, they can.

After this, it is just practice and perseverance – but don't give in during a weak moment and put a nappy or pull-up back on. It will simply confuse them. You have credited them with the intelligence and ability to do this – so be supportive (even if it kills you) and stick with it. Soon, potty visits will be as natural a part of their day to them as naps and meal times – part of the whole jigsaw you have been building since their birth.

Getting it right

Children who thrive on a By The Clock approach tend to also respond well to the idea of reward-based training. The idea that, 'if I do this well, then this will happen' fits nicely into their idea of predictability and stability.

Therefore, for this approach, star charts or sticker charts work well. You could vary this – some parents have a 'potty box' with small treats in it, to be offered when a wee or poo is produced (nothing for a 'try' – they have to produce something!). Some parents even create a special song which they sing in praise to their child when a successful potty visit has been achieved. Whatever it is, make it consistent – don't run out of chocolate buttons or forget the words to your special song – stick to your side of the deal.

Another good strategy is that, after the first few days when your child is consistently making successful potty attempts, start to move the potty closer to the bathroom. Gradually move it little by little, and then eventually put it in the bathroom once you feel your child has the control to make it when the urge comes.

You could, if you have only an upstairs bathroom or simply a large house, leave one potty downstairs for wees – but maybe insist that poos be done in the main bathroom, to introduce the idea of moving on to the big toilet.

Extra tips for success

In order to not disrupt your child's existing daytime routine of sleeping and eating, don't put them down for their daytime nap without a nappy – at first. For the first fortnight or so, put them in a pull-up for their nap and then give it a go when they are confident during their awake hours.

Let them get used to a special plastic-lined cushion around the house, so that they will accept sitting on it in the car when you venture out.

Once they are confident around the house about actually using the potty, but sometimes still forget, use a small kitchen timer set for every couple of hours. When the timer rings, it's potty time!

And consider drawing up a chart for yourself, to record 'hits' and 'misses' and when they occurred – it will help you adjust their routine to suit 'danger' times of day, and to more accurately predict when they might need to 'go'.

> ❝ Mine got a chocolate button every time they managed to go in the potty!
>
> Annie, mother of Tom, 14, and Olivia, 10 ❞

> ❝ Reward brothers and sisters with a sweet or a sticker as well as the potty training child – this encourages your toddler to 'go' because the siblings are willing them on! But reduce the level of praise slowly after about a week so that it becomes just a normal part of their behaviour. Remove rewards for weeing after about a week, and only offer a reward for doing a poo.
>
> Emma, mother of Aisha, seven, Anisa, four, and Omar, two ❞

GENTLY DOES IT

Getting started

The whole premise of the child-centred Gently Does It approach is that, since potty training is a developmental milestone in the same way that walking, talking and eating is, once you have introduced the potty and related tasks to your child, you should leave them to use it when they are developmentally ready to do so. They will, in effect, train themselves.

If you follow this route you are essentially putting your child in charge of when and how to train. There is no schedule to follow – the child sets the pace.

Children who have reached this decision for themselves typically get the hang of potty or toilet training quite easily. Indeed, this approach is a growing trend in Western society. An American study published in the April 2003 issue of *Pediatrics* reported that starting intensive toilet training (defined as asking a child more than three times a day to 'go') before 27 months simply lengthened the months of training it took for a child to be successful.

Some people even feel that potty training before this time isn't even potty training at all – it's just 'catching wee and poo'.

T. Berry Brazelton originally designed the child-centred approach in the early 1960s because he felt that other, more parent-led, methods were resulting in children failing at toilet training, refusing the toilet, suffering severe constipation and smearing their stools. He thought these techniques were pushing children before they were ready, and wanted to offer a gentler and more gradual approach.

If you think about it, the whole process of learning to be clean and dry is very complex. It involves the child:

- Being aware of the pressure sensations in their bowel or bladder
- Making the connection between these and what's happening inside their body
- Learning to respond to these by going to the potty
- Knowing how to remove clothes, and sit comfortably on the seat
- Being able to hold their urges until they are in position

So if you have decided to wait until your child is good and ready, and you feel that this is the time because they have indicated a desire to do it, how can you help them?

Firstly, introduce a potty chair – the larger commode styles feel more accommodating for an older toddler. Ask them to sit on it when fully clothed and when you are using the loo. Maybe talk or read a story to them while they are on it.

Then sit them on the potty chair with just a nappy on, after about a week of doing it fully clothed. If they soil their nappy, tip the contents into the chair and explain that this is where it goes. Take them to the chair two or three times a day.

After a few days, begin removing the nappy for short periods of time while keeping the potty chair close by. Encourage your child to use it independently.

Getting it right

The 'big breakthrough' – when your child sits on their potty naked and does something in it – is supposed to happen spontaneously. It is more likely to happen if they are naked on their bottom and the chair is somewhere obvious. They should think that using the potty is their idea, not yours!

Gentle reminders are ok, but telling your child outright to use the potty goes against this approach. All you focus on initially is waiting for them to decide to use the potty. You can wait to tackle subjects like flushing and washing hands until a later stage, when they show an interest in them.

Extra tips for success

Although older children often complete a Gently Does It approach with very little fuss – they do, after all, have superior bowel and bladder control, fine motor skills and verbal understanding than a younger baby – this is not a quick-fire method. Many children will be more than 30 months old before they are reliably successful. So don't stress about the timeline – remember, you are passing the control of this learning to your child, and empowering them to teach themselves.

Privacy is sometimes more of an issue for an older toddler, especially if they are trying to do a poo. Don't worry if they want to be alone in the bathroom – just make sure they cannot lock themselves in, and give them some space.

Some older toddlers do better sitting 'backwards' on an adult loo or larger potty, straddling it. Boys often find it easier to point their willy downwards this way. They can even rest a book or toy on the cistern bit of the loo.

If your child is already in pre-school or nursery, ask the caregivers to tell you about their daytime toileting experiences, and to help you with your approach.

> " My eldest child was a nightmare – I started far too early. Starting at two for boys I think is too soon. We struggled for months and still had accidents for a couple of years afterwards. So from him, I learned not to push it or even suggest it until the individual child was ready, and that seemed to work for the next four!
>
> Anton, mother of Jake, 10, Eleanor, eight, Buzz, seven, Lara, five and Bibi, three "

> " Because we had learned with Joe to wait until he was ready, we didn't even bring the subject up with his little brother Eddie. Then suddenly he requested to use the toilet last month. Great timing as we were on holiday so I had Andy around to help. We were happy to wait for him to initiate

the process this time – like Joe, it was peer influence that triggered it, we guess; Eddie wanted to be like his big brother.

Kate, mother of Joe, five, and Eddie, three **99**

Girls' Guide

- Girls often respond well to the more adventurous designs of potties, if you're feeling flush (excuse the pun). There are 'magic' ones with a design in the bowl that changes shape or colour when fluid hits it, and musical ones that play sound.

- You can also help avoid clothing battles by putting girls in loose dresses while potty training. They allow for quick action when needed, and more chance of her coping without your help.

Boys' Basics

- In the first days, let your child run around with a bare bottom. He is used to feeling a sensation of wetness in his nappy, but will not necessarily understand exactly which bit the wee comes out of. He needs to see it coming out.

- Most boys will want to sit on the potty at first. Don't push them to wee standing up – let them adapt to the potty first, and then maybe let them see Daddy or older brothers weeing standing up and make the decision to try this themselves.

" There is no need to be too prescriptive with whatever method of potty training you choose — the important thing is to go with a method that you feel is right for you and your child and that you will be able to stick with. There is nothing more confusing for the child or frustrating for the parent if the approach to potty training is constantly changed, resulting in no real progress. If you decide that whatever method you have chosen is not working then stop: have a break — think about why it didn't work — and restart when you feel more confident and have a clear plan of action. "

June Rogers, continence expert

Tackling the Toilet – and Bathroom Behaviour

❝ You can stand up in front of a bunch of four-year-olds and just say "toilet", and they'll start laughing.

Charlie Williams, footballer and comedian ❞

Why use the toilet? After all, most toilets are designed specifically for adults, right? Why make an infant or toddler use a contraption that is totally out of scale for them, that can't be transported or moved to a convenient location, that can be fallen into and that makes scary noises when operated? Why not just wait until they get bigger, and let them use a nice pint-sized potty in the meantime?

There are a few good reasons why toilets have to be tackled, whether it be sooner or later:

- You can't offer your child their preferred potty everywhere you go.

- If you are away from home, at a friend's house, in a shopping centre or on holiday, they might sometimes need to use an adult toilet.

- You might have decided that potties are an unnecessary stage in toilet training – why bother when they can go straight to the desired 'end result'?

❝ I didn't bother with potties as I thought I would just have to train them again to use the toilet. I bought a little mini seat that sat inside the big one.

Barbara, mother of Kate and Victoria **❞**

However, whether you and your child are going from potty to toilet or straight to toilet, they may well be hesitant in tackling this stage in their development. After all, it is large and high from the ground – imagine having to climb onto a loo which comes up to your chest. To cap it all, it has a big hole in it, and they have to suspend their delicate bits over cavernous and water-filled depths from which goodness knows what scary monsters might emerge ...

In addition to all of this, using the adult toilet usually marks a stage of independence which goes hand-in-hand with adult expectations about bathroom hygiene, cleanliness and safety issues.

On the plus side, using toilets from the start means you save money on buying several potties for home and away; it removes the chance that a child will confuse potties with toys sometimes, which makes potty training more difficult; and it gets rid of the task of emptying potties, dumping their contents and cleaning and sanitising afterwards.

Certain safety and hygiene issues are common to all training approaches, so we'll cover these first.

BATHROOM SAFETY

The main issues relating to children and bathroom safety are:

- Risk of being in proximity to water
- Risk of falling
- Risk of illness via germs and bacteria

To tackle the water issue, it is a good idea to establish a rule that plugs only go in baths or in sinks when an adult is present. Teach your child as early as possible that on taps 'blue means cold' and 'red means hot' - and that they may only use the cold tap when they are on their own.

For younger and adventurous bathroom users, it may be wise to invest in a toilet seat lock which can only be opened when you are there – although once you are properly established in your attempts to promote toilet use, this will be a deterrent you will not want. Therefore, once toilet use is being encouraged, equip your loo instead with a tight-fitting toilet insert and a small step or set of steps, and make a rule that children are not left unsupervised in the bathroom if the insert and steps are not in place.

There is an array of different designs of toilet insert available to you – when making your decision, look for features that indicate good quality. These are:

- A seat that is sturdy and well built

- A seat that is comfy, with some padding

- A seat with a splash guard for little boys, to help prevent 'over-shoots'

- A seat which can be adjusted to the exact size of the hole in your toilet seat

- You might also want to get one with handles on the sides which the child can steady themselves on.

A variation on this is the kind of toilet seat that fits permanently onto your toilet like a standard seat, but that also incorporates a second, smaller, pull-down version in the lid which can be unclipped for your child to use, and then put away in the lid when the toilet is for adult use.

The advantage to these is neatness – no bathroom cluttered with plastic inserts – and the fact that some children view these as 'more grown-up' and therefore are encouraged to use them. The main disadvantage is that it is fixed – so it cannot be used for different toilets or taken out for the day. Because of this, many parents find these excellent for use at grandparents' houses where the need for varied use is not as great, but use the plastic removable kind at home.

Also, you can buy inserts which are in four foldable sections, and therefore pack away into a small carry bag. I would recommend these – they fit easily and discreetly into a nappy bag or under a buggy or even into a handbag, and can be used on public toilets or on friends' toilets. So much better than carting a full-sized insert around under your arm.

> **66** Some advice I always give if people ask is not to bother with potties but to go straight onto the toilet if at all possible. Callum was very attached to his potty and refused to go on the loo for ages, which was quite a problem in the end. With the other two going straight onto the toilet, it meant no spillages with the kids trying to empty their own potties – not good for your carpets!
>
> Sharon, mother of Callum, six, Vincent, five, and Lauren, four **99**

Is your bathroom child-friendly?

As well as ensuring safety and comfort on the loo itself, it is also a good idea to look at the whole of your bathroom from a toddler's perspective. So:

- Make sure the toilet paper or wipes are within a child's arm's reach. The usual toilet dispenser may be fine for you, but might mean that your child has to lean over to grab it, which might cause them to topple and fall off.

- Teach your child that their step stool can be used in front of the sink too, for hand-washing, and make sure there are soaps and a clean towel within their reach.

- Some companies make foaming soap in fun dispensers, or bar soaps with toys embedded in them – these can encourage hand-washing initially, although it is cost-effective to move them onto ordinary soap as soon as you can.

- Be aware of the lock on your bathroom door – can a child easily lock themselves in from the inside? If so, disable it temporarily, and maybe add a bolt high up on the door for adult use.

- Make sure any detergents, cleaners, bleach products, razors, scissors or drinkable toiletries are locked away.

- Replace glasses with paper or plastic cups.

- Lower water temperature to a maximum 48°C.

- Be aware that steps and toilets can be used to climb higher – make sure you have secure window locks fitted.

- Be careful what you throw in the bathroom bin – no razor blades, hair colouring products, or medications.

Germ warfare

There will always be germs in the bathroom, particularly with a young child about! Trying to eliminate them completely is futile and creates unnecessary stress.

What you should aim to do is reduce the likelihood of your child – and the rest of the family – coming into close contact with them needlessly, and encourage good hygiene habits for everyone to follow so the whole family stays healthy.

Here are some basic bathroom rules:

- **Teach your child to wipe themselves**. This can be something of a challenge for young children with undeveloped fine motor skills. Explain to toddlers and older children why it is important – and use simple language, telling them it stops bad smells and itching, and keeps new underwear clean and smart.

- **Flush**. It stops germs from building up.

- **Wash hands**. Every time, for wees and poos alike. Use soap, lather, rinse well and dry. Try creating a colourful child version of the 'Now Please Wash Your Hands' mantra we were taught as children – older children can help you design and draw a poster which you can laminate and put near the sink.

Children are always fascinated by anything containing water, and by anything they can climb on – so experiments with bathroom mountaineering and stuffing things into the loo are inevitable.

What you can do is keep things as clean as possible. Keep the toilet (including under the lid) and surrounding surfaces clean – keep some disposable disinfectant cleaning wipes in a locked cupboard nearby, and give everything a quick wipe whenever you go in there. It takes less time and effort than getting out bottles and cloths, and will therefore get done more frequently.

Use a toilet block to combat germs that build up when children forget to flush – make sure it is one that is used in the cistern rather than one that dangles enticingly under the rim.

Good bathroom hygiene at home also makes it easier to teach good hygiene in public toilets. You might teach your toddler how to use a disposable toilet seat, or to use toilet paper on the seat.

Another thing worth noting on the hygiene front is that different cultures require different hygiene methods in the bathroom. Muslims, for instance, traditionally require that children learn to wash their bottoms with water using their left hand, rather than using toilet paper. Some Muslim households have a small water shower in the bathroom for this purpose. In traditional households, smooth stones are also used. Many Muslims in Western countries have adapted this practice and encourage children to use a disposable moist toilet wipe instead – when they go to school or away from home, they carry a small pack of these with them.

This is probably good practice for children of any culture – and something to be aware of when your child starts bringing home friends who may need such toiletries on offer.

Now – once you have established your basic bathroom ''elf 'n' safety' rules, you can refer to your chosen Potty Training approach for more tips.

EARLY DAYS

Top toilet tips

The best thing you can do when starting potty training with a very young child is to fully establish those 'cue sounds', such as 'psss' and 'hmmm'. Once a baby has become accustomed to these cues when doing wees and poos in a pot, they can then quickly become the cue when the child is held over an adult toilet.

Some parents even start with the toilet in the very early days, even when the child is a few weeks old – the disadvantage to this is that it limits how responsive you can be when your baby is weeing every few minutes – that's a lot of trips to the bathroom, especially if you have to negotiate a flight of stairs!

However, when your baby has slightly better bladder control, it is worth trying to 'catch' at least some of your baby's efforts in the adult toilet, because they will then begin to recognise this – and any other unfamiliar toilets – as a 'potty' or acceptable place to 'go'.

As your child grows and becomes more able to control their urges, rather than relying on you to get the timing right, you can then start to practise with them sitting on an insert in the toilet itself, rather than being dangled over the top of it. This then quickly leads to full use of the toilet, without the need to go through the potty stage.

Bathroom battles

The big issue for some children who have been used to an Early Days approach to potty training is that they have grown accustomed to close bodily contact with a parent while doing wees and poos. They often rely not only on the adult's help with timing, but also on the sense of security and reassurance that comes with such close contact.

When the time comes for the child to begin to use the big toilet independently, they can sometimes feel exposed and frightened, even though they are used to viewing the toilet as a receptacle for their waste.

It is therefore worth making extra efforts to give your child a real sense of security when using the big toilet. Make sure that set of steps is the right height to give them a good 'pushing' platform. When buying a toilet insert, go for one with small handles on the sides, to give your child something to hold onto. Put some board books or small toys in a basket which are just for the bathroom – something to hold their interest, take away their nerves, and give them an incentive to try doing it themselves.

Also, reward their efforts to judge their own needs, and to follow them through, with a sticker chart or some kind of reward or praise – the chances are they will still be very young in comparison to other children who are using the toilet for the first time, so recognise their early abilities and let them know how proud you are.

> **"** We held Kitty over the big toilet when she was very young, if we were in time or close by – if not, we held her over her potty bowl instead, but often let her see us tip the contents down the big toilet afterwards. She was only about 14 months when she was happy to sit on the big toilet with an insert on it – we bought one with little handles on the sides to give her a bit of extra security and to help her balance.
>
> Mary-anne, mother of Kitty, three, and Finn, 11 months **"**

NON-STOP BOT

Top toilet tips

With the Non-Stop Bot approach, speed is of course of the essence. And if they are successful with it, most parents can't find much to complain about! But if there is one slight issue with this approach, it is that this very need for speed does require a child to take on a lot of new experiences, responsibilities and instructions all at once.

So, just as your child has – within days and sometimes even hours – got the hang of what a potty is for and how to reach it in time, they have to embark on yet another learning curve and make all that new knowledge apply to the big toilet, which is probably further away and is certainly a whole lot more intimidating than their usual potty.

Now, you could decide that, if you are going to potty train in a very short period of time, you will simply skip the potty and go straight for the toilet. This is not impossible – but be warned, it is likely that you will have a lot more accidents to clear up than if you include a potty stage. This is because you are using an approach which bombards a child with everything all at once – you are not doing this over a prolonged period during which they have the chance to become gradually accustomed to the adult toilet and to reaching the bathroom.

What is more usual when following a Non-Stop Bot approach is to start off with your child using a potty, and then gradually move that potty to the bathroom, aiming for a stage when they can consistently control their bladder and bowel for long enough that nearly all wees and poos are done in the bathroom, rather than the living areas of the house.

Only at this stage, when the bathroom has been established as 'the place to go', do you make the move to the toilet. And to make this as non-threatening as possible, make sure you are set up with steps and an insert and have followed the above 'child-friendly bathroom' checklist.

Bathroom battles

Because you might find that your Non-Stop Botter, having taken on so much so quickly, baulks at making this final step, you must do everything you can to make them feel at home on the adult toilet.

Big toilets are scary to little people because of:

- Their size – relative to your child
- Their shape – they are hollow and can be fallen into
- Their noise – the flush is loud and unfamiliar
- They splash – it feels cold and scary on the bottom

> 66 Oliver was afraid of the loo. He would refuse to do anything on it. We worked out it wasn't the toilet itself, but the 'drop' underneath the loo he was afraid of. So first we let him poo in his nappy, then onto a nappy, then we put the nappy in the loo and he pooed onto it in the loo, and then he was ok. But it took a lot of coaxing and patience.
>
> Clare, mother of Emma, six, Oliver, four, Evie, two and Hannah, two months 99

Bearing this in mind, you can do certain things to make these factors less of an issue. The size factor can be tackled with the steps, and with making sure that toilet paper isn't too great a stretch away. Get your child to sit a large teddy on the insert, and let them watch you on the loo to notice how you use your feet to balance.

The fact that the toilet is hollow and things disappear down it can be made into a bit of a fun experiment. Can they throw small bits of cereal in there, and practise flushing them away? Or some coloured ice cubes? Perhaps you can invent a little rhyme or song to sing when they 'say goodbye' to the wees and poos tipped in there from the potty. When you do all of this, let them practise flushing – this will help them get used to the noise of the flush and the action of the water in the bowl.

Finally, to stop splashing, simply put a couple of sheets of toilet paper down the bowl first. A couple only though – make sure your child doesn't think half a roll is required!

Then, when your child is ready to sit on the toilet, kneel down by them so that you are on their level. Hold them around the waist, initially. Maintain reassuring eye contact. As they become more confident, hold them with just one hand, and eventually let them sit alone, but remain at their level. In this way, they will progress to using the toilet independently, without you even in the room.

> **❝** Elliott used a potty once or twice early on, around 18 months, and then we had a holiday away where he was in the nude most of the time. He grasped it there himself using a big boy toilet.
>
> Victoria, mother of Elliott, six **❞**

BY THE CLOCK

Top toilet tips

By The Clock children tend to thrive on routine, and on fun ways of helping them to keep to that routine. For this approach, a 'toilet schedule' can be brilliantly effective. A toilet schedule is any system that helps a child get into the habit of using an adult toilet.

The method promotes *regular* toilet use – and because of this, it has the added bonus that accidents will tend to occur less frequently, because a child doesn't have the chance to get desperate. To do this:

- Prompt your child to use the toilet on a regular basis – every hour, for instance, and also at key times such as after waking, before bath time, after meals, or before leaving the house.

- Don't just ask – the answer will invariably be 'no'! Phrase it so that it is a positive but non-optional invitation: 'It's time to go to the toilet – let's go!' or 'Time to see if a wee or a poo is ready'.

If, once you get to the toilet, your child doesn't need to 'go', it doesn't matter. Say, 'Well done for trying – let me know if you need one in a little while.' Equally, if they have an accident outside of your 'schedule', don't make a fuss: just say, 'Never mind, next time we'll get to the toilet in time'.

And if they spontaneously visit the toilet between allotted schedule times, this is of course fantastic – it shows that they are beginning to rely on their own urges, rather than the clock.

Bathroom battles

Although By The Clock children are fantastic at instructions and commands, making things a whole lot easier when learning a new skill, they can sometimes become over-reliant on routine and on an adult directing them.

So, what is essential here is that you only use your toilet schedule up to the point when your child has essentially become accustomed to going to the bathroom every so often, and is consistently reaching it on time. At this stage, wean them off the schedule and throw away the timer – you need them to be confident enough to rely on their own feelings. After all, if they have a play date at another child's house, there may not be an adult around who has the time or the inclination to issue toilet reminders every hour.

The goal is that the schedule makes going to the toilet an instinctive, 'second nature' activity – it should not become an end in itself to follow a timetable. Once your child has got the idea, praise them if they suggest a toilet visit on their own, and start to lengthen times between scheduled visits until the reminders are no longer needed.

> We were great ones for sticker charts in our family. The children all designed theirs themselves, with a bit of help from us! Rebecca, I think I remember, had a princess castle one. Ashley liked animals and did a jungle one. And Vincent still has his one: it's a spaceship with planets. We let them pick out their own stickers. When they made the move from potties to the toilet, we moved the charts to the back of the bathroom door and kept the stickers next to the towels, and they added a sticker for every successful visit!
>
> Tom, father of Rebecca, nine, Ashley, six, and Vincent, three

GENTLY DOES IT

Top toilet tips

The good thing about children who tackle the toilet at a slightly later age is that they are already more independent, and also taller and stronger physically.

Many parents who opt for a Gently Does It approach decide to leave out the potty stage entirely. After all, many older toddlers look slightly uncomfortable perched on a tiny potty, and many decide for themselves that they want to copy Mummy or Daddy and go to the loo the 'grown-up way'.

Whether your child is going from potty to toilet or straight to toilet, there are a couple of challenges that arise purely from the fact that your child is not a small infant.

Firstly, these are children who are used to being on the move, and who probably dislike staying in one place for very long.

Secondly, at this stage their minds are active too – they are less easily persuaded or distracted, and more likely to want to assert their own will, even if that means getting up mid-poo to reach something on the other side of the bathroom or to fetch something from their bedroom.

A good mantra for Gently Does It parents is this: 'entertainment makes it easy!'

Use the fact that your child is more advanced and further developed – keep books, puzzles and other self-contained toys in a box or basket in the bathroom for use during toilet time. These will help your child stay patient – and stay still – while they 'go', and will also make the whole idea of going into the bathroom and using the toilet a more attractive option.

Some parents even restrict certain in-demand toys for use solely at toilet time, as it keeps the child's interest in those things fresh, and prevents them from getting bored.

Books – picture books and ones that can be read together – also have the added advantage of reinforcing your child's love of stories and learning and helps you to develop their reading skills at the same time!

Bathroom battles

Another issue which can raise its head for Gently Does It families is the temptation to think that, because your child is slightly older and is already becoming independent in other areas such as feeding themselves and playing, you can rely on them to use the toilet with little or no help.

But think about it – when your child learned to feed themselves, you had to show them a spoon or fork, and let them watch you use one, before you let them loose on their meals by herself. The same is true of toilet use. Remember how big a toilet is, even for a three- or four-year-old. Have a few practice sessions where you ask them to practise climbing onto the toilet or toilets in your own home. Help them get up and down a few times. Let girls watch their mothers and boys watch their fathers.

And don't be afraid to let them be creative! If your child feels comfortable sitting back-to-front on the loo and steadying themselves on the cistern, let them. At first, it's all about overcoming the fear – you will have time later to adjust the actual technique.

66 When Ellie was starting to use the big toilet, we had spent a couple of weeks where she was using her potty but it had to be in the bathroom. She still wasn't that keen on actually making the move to the toilet. But what clinched it was that we put a little CD player in the bathroom, on a low stool where she could reach it, and had a CD in it that played fairy stories and music. She turned it on when she wanted to 'go'. It also kept her sitting there long enough to do poos! Now we're doing the same with Pip.

Karen, mother of Ellie, six, and Pippa, four 99

66 Both boys have skipped using the potty. By the time they were ready they were big enough physically to manage getting on and off, and old enough not to be scared of falling down the toilet! They also enjoyed flushing and washing. That's been great — no slopping out duties for Andy and me!

Kate, mother of Joe, five, and Eddie, three 99

Girls' Guide

- Encourage girls right from the beginning to wipe from front to back after a poo. This prevents bacteria from causing a urine infection.

- Teach girls that they have to sit well back on the seat and 'aim down' – otherwise you tend to get a leak onto the seat or down the outside of the toilet. A good aim isn't just for the boys!

Boys' Basics

- Encourage boys to aim their wee into the toilet – do 'target practice' and make it fun. Many little boys get distracted and let their stream wander onto the floor, toilet lid or washing basket ... getting into the habit of doing a quick wipe round the floor and seat area with a disinfectant wipe every time you go in there yourself, just in case, is probably a good back-up.

- Once boys start to learn how to wee standing up in front of an adult toilet, you have the risk of injury to willies. If they learn using a stool, they will be high enough to avoid this, however, if, like many boys, they 'hook' their willy over the rim of the loo, explain to them that the seat or lid of the toilet can fall down. Get them to practise holding their 'spare' hand in front of them, just in case they need to catch a falling lid. You could also install a hook or suction cup to hold the lid in place, or even remove it temporarily. It is also good practice to make sure a boy's willy is not actually touching the toilet rim, where it will come into contact with germs.

❝ Make using the toilet fun! Use 'targets' in the toilet for little boys to aim at. A few drops of food colouring in the cistern will change the colour of every flush — make a game of what colour the flush will be the next time they use the toilet.

Bottom wiping — again make this fun. Introduce the concept early on and help the child practise reaching round to their bottom — sticking a pretend animal tail onto the back of their clothes and encouraging the child to reach round and pull it off is one way.

❞

June Rogers, continence expert

Out and About

66 Happiness is like peeing in your pants. Everyone can see it, but only you can feel the warmth.

Anonymous 99

A toilet is a toilet, right? When you've got to go, you've got to go... and it doesn't really matter which receptacle you use. Unfortunately for many children, this is not the case. Even children who are very reliable and confident using either the potty or the toilet at home struggle to transfer those skills when they are out and about.

In fact, venturing out of the house at all with a small child and no nappy is enough to make most parents quake in their boots. A simple trip to town becomes a navigational nightmare, which involves having to make a mental map of every available 'potty stop' along the high street.

Emergency stops in public toilets range from almost acceptable to downright grotty, and often require armfuls of antibacterial wipes and toilet seat covers. A journey in the car can lead to soggy car seats and sudden cries of, 'I need to go – *now*!' when you are stuck in the middle of three lanes of stationary traffic. And if you should even contemplate going *on holiday* – planes, airports, trains, ferries! – and leaving the trusty nappies and pull-ups behind, you are either in line for the Intrepid Parent of the Year Award, or just blissfully optimistic.

Actually, it is quite possible to 'manage' a child's newly found toilet skills when away from home – it just involves a little preparation and a strong disposition. Firstly, let's cover the main areas of 'out and about' toileting challenges that are common to any approach.

FIRST TRIPS OUT

Family and friends

It is likely that some of your very first adventures away from home will involve trips to the houses of family and friends. This is a good idea, because they are likely to be fairly familiar environments, and the adults are likely to be sensitive to your child's needs and nerves, and will help you reassure them. Also, you have some flexibility. You can bring a familiar potty or toilet insert along, and maybe a favourite toy or book.

Before you go, explain to the friend or relative how you handle accidents at home, and ask them to maintain a positive attitude if things go wrong. Tell them you will clear up, of course. And ask about any special bathroom issues you might need to know – for instance, a very loud toilet flush, a wonky toilet seat, or a hard-to-reach light or toilet paper roll.

Lastly, be aware that medicines, razors, cleaning products and other hazards may not be as securely locked away as they are at home – accompany your child, and explain to them not to touch any belongings other than the toilet paper, soap, tap and towel in somebody else's bathroom.

Then simply follow your home routine, making sure you issue a few more reminders than usual.

Childminders and nurseries

Most childminders and carers will be only too pleased that your child is becoming more independent. If your child goes to a nursery, talk to them about their policies and how you can help your child adjust. If your child will need to be able to use a big toilet, for instance, you can practise at home.

If it's a childminder, you will probably need to get them on board from the start of potty training. If they refuse to participate in potty training, think twice about letting your child stay there. Good childminders will take this in their stride, and should actually become a second bow to your arrow in the quest for your child's independence.

> 66 I always continue and help with a child's potty training when they are with me. How could you not? It just becomes part of the routine when they are at my house. I talk to the parents about how they are doing it at home, and try to keep to something similar. And actually, when they see the other children using the toilet quite normally, it helps them to feel that there is nothing to be worried about and that it's just what everyone does.
>
> Nikki, childminder and mother of George, six 99

> 66 When Joe was not having much success with potty training at home, I was still pretty confident that he had some kind of control – his pre-school wouldn't take nappy-clad kids so I had been sending him in pants and crossing my fingers, and he never had a single accident there!
>
> Kate, mother of Joe, five, and Eddie, three 99

Local loos

A good way to follow on from trips to familiar locations is to make small, manageable trips into town. Initially, you could try to time your outing so that your child doesn't need to go at all while you are out, but you will soon need to gradually introduce the idea of 'going' on an unfamiliar toilet.

When you do this, try to pick smaller, cosier toilets at first. Using a toilet in a bookshop or coffee shop is a better first experience of public loos than 20 busy stalls in the local shopping centre. Work your way up to this gradually.

PUBLIC LOOS

We all know that the hygiene standards in public toilets vary quite a bit. What you need to do – quickly, because your child will probably be twisting their legs in knots by the time you get there – is make a basic assessment of what will be required to make them comfortable.

Judge the queue. If your little one is desperate, ask other adults if you can cut in – most people will let small children go to the front of the queue.

In the cubicle, use a toilet insert or toilet cover if you have one. If not, you may need to help your child stay stable on the seat. You can crouch down and hold them round the waist, or even kneel on the floor so that they can put their feet on your thighs to push. You can use disposable seat covers or loo roll to protect your knees!

One of the biggest issues reported by parents in public loos is noise. The main culprits are noisy flushes – especially the automatic kind that goes off when you are still 'going' – and hand dryers (my daughter Evie, six, still shrinks away from these).

But there are things you can do to reduce the noise:

- Drape a piece of toilet paper over the automatic flush sensor before helping your child sit on the toilet. Even better, keep some plasters in your bag and stick one over the sensor. You can even buy a 'Flush-Stopper' device which does the same thing. Automatic flushes are more erratic if a small child is on the toilet, because their frames are too small for the sensor to register correctly.

- Avoid toilets with lots of cubicles.

- Carry an MP3 player with some of your child's favourite songs on it, and 'plug them in' while they are in the toilets.

- Take your own paper towels to dry hands so your child doesn't have to go near the hand blowers.

- Look out for family rooms which usually have just one toilet, rather than a row of them. If you have to use toilets with lots of stalls, try to choose one that has unoccupied stalls next to it to keep noise at a distance.

- If they don't like the flush, let your child stand outside the open door by the sink while you flush for them.

It is also worthwhile teaching children some basic safety ground rules for when they are in a public toilet:

- Explain that while public loos are not scary, everyone needs to be careful in them. 'Big girls and boys' have to be sensible, to keep themselves safe from germs, and from someone who might pretend to be a nice person but isn't.

- Establish a rule early on that your child must go with you to the toilet and never run off. If they insist on privacy, you can stand outside holding the door. Don't let small children turn the lock, especially in a cubicle that cannot be climbed over.

- Tell your child not to speak to other people in a public toilet unless it is an emergency – and then to look for another parent with small children.

- Teach your child that a toilet area is not a play area. They should not play with the toilet flushes, the sinks or the toilet paper.

- Teach them germ safety. Show them how to use soap and lather properly, how to clean under fingernails, how to rinse well and how to dry. Get them to sing a short song or rhyme under their breath while they are doing it, to make sure they wash long enough – 'Happy Birthday' is a good one.

CAR TRAVEL

Once you are truly out and about, you will inevitably have to negotiate car travel without nappies. And what you can't deny is that little people still learning new toilet skills cannot 'hold on'. Telling a two-year-old to keep their legs crossed until the next service station in 20 miles is neither practical nor fair.

The best way to tackle this is to be prepared – it takes all (okay, most of) the fear out of it.

Good car equipment might include:

- **Wet wipes** – lots!

- **A transportable or inflatable potty** – put two plastic bags in it, in case one splits. After use, just tie them up ready for disposal.

- **Clean clothes** – for your child, although a spare pair of trousers for you might come in handy too.
- **Plastic bags** – large sealable ones for wet clothes.
- **Nappy sacks** – for disposing of solid waste.

Most parents also like to put something underneath their child in case of accidents, which are most likely to happen if a child falls asleep on a long journey. This might be a special fitted waterproof car seat cover, an adapted cushion, or anything else that protects – we used one of those disposable mini bed sheets tucked between bottom and seat.

" We always put a plastic potty with a lid on the back car seat, in the gap between our children's two car seats. If one of them needs to go, we pull over to the side of the road, unbuckle them and let them sit on the potty in the middle. This is useful if it's pouring down with rain outside, or you're on a dangerous motorway hard shoulder – nobody even has to get out of the car.

Jen, mother of Lucas, four, and Edmund, two "

" We will admit to using old McDonald's drink cups for emergency boys' wees in the car. Never works for girls though – mine is always too shy and sensible!

Annie, mother of Tom, 14, and Olivia, 10 "

PLANES, TRAINS AND 'MOVING LOOS'

This kind of travel is easier than you might think. At least there is a toilet close at hand, and clearly signposted.

What you need to do to make it easier, though, is talk to your child beforehand about the kinds of toilets we find on planes and trains. Tell them that the space is cramped, and sometimes the vehicle jolts or tips - but tell them that you will help them balance, and try to have a fun, adventurous attitude.

Another thing to warn them about with aeroplane travel is the noisy flush - seeing the hole open and hearing the sudden suction of a plane toilet can be incredibly frightening for some children, and might even set them back in their toilet training. Better to move them away from the toilet to stand in the doorway while you flush, blocking their view with your body.

> 66 I've got a tip for the beach when they need a wee. Bury the bucket, and put a nappy bag in it to line it – and hey presto, you have a very discreet loo!
>
> Annie, mother of Tom, 14, and Olivia, 10 99

YOUR SIGNALS

It's easy to get very stressed if you are accompanying an unpredictable small person with unreliable bladder and bowel control. And yes, a child who is away from home, taking in new sights and sounds, distracted, and with a parent who may also be distracted and forget to issue reminders, is of course more likely than usual to have an accident.

But – remember, there are worse things. And even the most catastrophic of accidents can be dealt with if you have a plastic bag and enough wipes.

So try to relax. You need to send positive vibes to your child. Remember also that you will pass on any negative feelings you may have about public toilets if you are anxious – by all means be hygienic, but if you enter a public loo as if it were a nuclear installation, frantically spreading protective sheets over every surface and spraying your child with antibac from head to toe, they may well pick up on your own apprehension. Safety is what you are aiming for, not paranoia.

Now – let's look at some extra tips which will help you with your chosen potty training approach.

EARLY DAYS

Preparation

Because Early Days children are likely to be younger than most potty trainers, things have to be a bit more flexible when it comes to leaving the house.

Of course it will depend what stage you have reached as to what you can expect. For a child who has been following this approach for some time, it might be reasonable to expect that they can follow their usual cues, and you can use a small potty, pot or a public toilet to help them 'go'.

For a younger infant, or if you are going somewhere inflexible such as a large family event, it might be wiser to use a nappy or pull-up just for the day. While this might go against what you are trying to achieve, it is better to make the odd exception than to lead your child into a situation where they feel they have failed, and make them reluctant to carry on that special 'team effort' you have created.

Top toilet tips

If you are determined to help your child use a big toilet or public toilet, there are things you can do to make it easier:

- Take your child's underwear and trousers or skirt off before you start, if you can. Then lift your child and hold them over the toilet, facing the back – this gives you more room; is a familiar 'pose' from home; and helps them to focus on 'going', rather than being distracted by what's happening outside the door.

- Another approach is to sit on the toilet yourself, as far back as you can, and then put your child in front of you. This provides a reassuring place to lean back on, and you can hold their legs to steady them.

> **❝❝** We flew to Spain with Lola, and for the actual journey we put her in a nappy. I couldn't rely on getting her into the aeroplane loo on time if there was a queue or if the seatbelt signs were on – and didn't fancy holding over her the pot in full view of the other passengers. But as soon as we got to our apartment we took it off and went off to find the bathroom together, and sure enough, she weed

as soon as we used her cues. When we were on the beach, we took a few nappies and had her 'go' onto those, and then just put them in a nappy bag. Actually, many Spanish children are trained early anyway, so our way of doing things was probably less unusual there than back home!

Jane, mother of Lola, one

"

NON-STOP BOT

Preparation

If your child has followed a very rapid approach to potty training, it is likely that they will not have had a long period of time to become used to toilets in all their shapes and forms, and may well be more nervous than a child who has followed a gradual approach.

In order to reassure them, there are a couple of things you can do:

- Start to take your child into public toilets when you are out and about, even if they don't need to go. Let them see you use a public toilet, even if you just go in to wash your hands and check the mirror. They will become used to the noises and the procedure involved.

- Create a 'potty path' with them. Get them involved in thinking about where the 'pit stops' are in your local town. On longer trips, check maps and make sure you know where you can find service stations, or fast food outlets with toilets.

Top toilet tips

Some parents think that potty training while away on holiday is madness. Some Non-Stop Botters, however, think that this is the ideal time to do a crash course in toilet training.

Their argument is that potty or toilet training away from home is easier for some children precisely because a new setting is an easier place in which to begin new habits. When they are on holiday, families tend to feel more relaxed and routines are looser, which makes the whole procedure much less stressful for your toddler. If you are going away with friends who have slightly older children, your child might try to emulate them and impress the 'big children', which is a fantastic incentive.

On top of this, if you choose a warm location, your child can potter about in the nude a lot, with strategically placed potties, and this is much easier than fitting potty training into a wet and windy week in a British half-term!

66 I often suggest that once children are beyond that initial nappy/potty confusion stage, the best portable loo for little boys in the car is actually a nappy. I just had Luca wee onto a nappy, and due to the absorbency it was much easier to dispose of than nappy contents (even in the portable nappy bags) and less potentially messy than having him wee behind a tree. I take one in my bag on flights too, as I have a nightmare about us being stuck in our seat for ages due to

turbulence or something and him not being able to go!

Liat, mother of Luca, four

"

BY THE CLOCK

Preparation

Your child is probably quite proficient now at using a potty or toilet, and feels comfortable and secure within their usual toilet routine. The problem is – how do you help them to be flexible enough to adapt that routine outside the home?

Well, as long as you are prepared, it *is* still possible to maintain a semblance of your normal routine, even in the most unpredictable of circumstances:

- Before you go, pack anything that will reinforce the familiar and the comforting – a toilet insert, a favourite book or toy, a small towel from home. If they would like, perhaps they can help you create a special 'holiday' sticker chart decorated with buckets and spades and drawings of all the family, and even fill it in with small shells stuck on with glue ... whatever captures their imagination but keeps to their routine.

- If you have trouble remembering everything you usually do at home, make a list or a picture diagram for your child, and follow it through together. The routine becomes the backbone your child relies upon when all the other circumstances seem strange and possibly threatening.

Top toilet tips

Once you are there:

- Think about what you would be doing at home. If you normally encourage your child to go to the toilet on waking, or after breakfast, then make sure you do this on holiday too. It doesn't matter if it's a hotel bathroom, a potty outside a tent, or a stop by the side of the road – it's the timing that matters, not the location.

- Remember your 'toilet schedule'? Keep to it. Take enforced breaks if possible, every one to one-and-a-half hours, even if your child says they don't need to go. Make the whole family go too – 'Here we are, let's all get out and go and find the toilets'.

- Sing your usual 'toilet song' if you have one, continue to use that sticker chart, and offer your usual praise, even if you have a thousand things on your mind or have one ear on the tannoy ... it all makes a difference to maintaining their confidence.

> ❝ We often drive long distances for family holidays. We make a thing of planning for the journey; sticking little coloured stickers on our road map where we can stop for toilet breaks. One of the best countries we have found for easy road trips is France – the roads are a lot emptier than in England, and they have a very reliable system of 'aires', which are like service stations but much better. Most have big grassy picnic areas with tables, and you can stop and have a snack as well as a toilet stop. If the whole

family's doing it, the little ones just accept the need to stop too.

Tom, father of Rebecca, nine, Ashley, six, and Vincent, three

99

GENTLY DOES IT

Preparation

For Gently Does It children, the emphasis is on maintaining their desire to be independent and 'doing it themselves', while providing the back-up to help them do so without losing confidence in their abilities.

The advantage for these children is that they tend to be older, and are therefore easier to involve in catering for their own needs. They also find it easier to listen to explanations and instructions.

Many children who are 'later starters' and who have made the decision themselves that they want to potty train are quite concerned with the idea of only weeing and pooing in a certain place. They see Mummy or Daddy doing it at home, they decide to copy, they get used to their own potty and their own toilet, and they therefore conclude that home is where people wee and poo.

The idea that Mummy, Daddy or the child themselves might go to a different place to wee or poo is, to some, quite a leap. What if it doesn't work? What if it is scary? How do I do it? What you need to do is involve your child in *deciding* they *can* do it away from home too.

Top toilet tips

- Prepare them. Tell your child about going to a new place, with new toilets, but explain that you will still be there to help, and they will still have their toilet insert, or wipes, or whatever makes them feel safe.

- Take, if you can, a potty or insert they have used before.

- Consider telling them they can wear a pull-up or training pants if they want to – by doing this, you are giving them permission not to get it right, which takes the pressure off.

- Recognise that some children feel quite possessive about their wees and poos, and don't like to see them flushed away in a new place – ask them if they want to flush it, so you are giving them control.

- Don't make a fuss if an accident happens – let your child know that you realise you are asking them to make big changes, and that you are fine if they don't always get it right. Reassure them that 'everyone has accidents sometimes' and that it will all settle down as they get used to things.

- Older children can be taught to recognise the symbol for toilets at service stops, and use this to remind adults to stop – again, this empowers your child and shows that you trust them to take control sometimes.

66 Be careful that going backwards and forwards with nappies or pull-ups on or off, and a really laid-back approach to accidents, doesn't create problems. The child may get mixed messages which can be confusing and lead to behavioural issues. Have some clear boundaries and make sure your child knows them.

June Rogers, continence expert

99

66 We got ourselves into a right pickle with Cara. She was a late potty trainer – I was working full-time and there just didn't seem to be a good moment to start, so she ended up doing it when she was four. But I think that led into this problem that she is incredibly fussy about toilets – she has a fear of touching stuff. She's ok at home, but doesn't like using 'strange' loos; which is a problem on holiday! We try to play it down and not make a big deal of it, but I did find that if we let her use one of those antibac hand gel things, she is less worried about the whole thing.

Emma, mother of Cara, eight

99

Girls' Guide

- Teach girls to squat so that their feet and clothing are out of the way, so that they can 'go' outside if they have to. You can help her by showing her the right position, and supporting her as she squats.

- Often dads ask what they are supposed to do if they are out with their daughter and she has to use a public toilet. Some dads with younger toilet-training daughters will get them to use a potty in the back of the car or beside the car. Some look for disabled toilets which are unisex. Some ask a woman to check if the ladies toilet is empty, and then pop straight into a cubicle with their little girl – most women would not be offended by a dad doing this. And some tuck their daughter's head into their shoulder to restrict her vision, and head straight into a cubicle in the gents toilets – using wipes or handwash outside afterwards rather than hanging around to use the sinks. What you shouldn't do is ask someone you don't know to take your child into a ladies toilet for you. Stay with your child at all times.

Boys' Basics

- Although some parents insist potty training boys is harder than girls, boys do have a distinct advantage when it comes to being out and about – they can wee standing up! Get him used to discreetly weeing down a drain, or on a patch of grass, or next to a tree – sometimes weeing outside on a long journey is much more pleasant than using a dirty or run-down public toilet, and most people don't mind a toddler doing it if they are neat and tidy!

- Make sure this 'cavalier' attitude doesn't extend to wiping. Although boys are less at risk than girls if they don't wipe properly – because it is harder for the bacteria to enter the urinary tract – they will become sore and smelly if they don't. Wet wipes are a great option for on-the-move boys.

66 Try not to make a big deal of going out of the house – if your child sees you are anxious they will become anxious as well! There are lots of portable potties and toilet seats etc on the market which can make toileting on the go much easier. Also, if your child has just been taken out of nappies do not be tempted to put them back in 'just in case' as this causes confusion. **99**

June Rogers, continence expert

5

Night-time Control

<blockquote>
" I don't want to be a stinky poo poo girl; I want to be a happy flower child.

Drew Barrymore, actress "
</blockquote>

So things are going pretty well. You have been following your chosen approach, and your child is starting to get the hang of this toilet business – they can even manage fairly well out in the big wide world. You should feel more than a bit pleased with yourself – and with your child.

But you have one more battle to fight – and it's a big one. And that battle is going to be won – yes, won! – in the bedroom. It's time to tackle night-time dryness: the final hurdle in the potty training race.

IS IT REALLY MUCH HARDER THAN DAY-TIME TRAINING?

It's funny how many books and articles on potty and toilet training never really get around to fully dealing with night-times. They march you through the initial days, coax you through getting out of the house, and praise you when you have tackled the adult toilet … but when it comes to solid, practical advice on night-times, the advice peters out into wishy-washy comments such as 'this takes a little longer' and 'it just depends on the child'.

Some children are just fine making the move into nappy-free bedtimes. But of all the stages of potty training, this is the one which seems to throw up longer-term problems and doubts. And it is also the one area parents are less likely to talk about. Whereas most of us have thrown up our hands in mock despair or even cried piteously in front of our friends and other parents when day-time potty training has gone horribly wrong, there seem to be an awful lot of Mums and Dads out there who have older children either in pull-ups at night or wetting the bed on a regular basis – and who feel they cannot even mention it.

At its worst, it becomes a kind of 'family secret', which can even prevent children from going on sleepovers or families sharing holidays with friends – something socially unacceptable and somehow shaming. So – let's get this in perspective. We are dealing with small children. And by 'small', that does not just mean toddlers. Even a five- or a six-year-old is still a small, developing child. And small children need our help and patience, not our judgement and embarrassment.

Admittedly, having to tackle wet sheets and piles of washing every morning is wearing for the parent so it is easy to blow this out of proportion. But we are talking wee here, not serious illness or grave misbehaviour. Wee is an inconvenience, not a catastrophe.

WHEN SHOULD I BE CONCERNED?

It might help to look at the average ages by which children tend to be dry overnight. It is a lot later than you might expect. Experts do not expect a child to be dry at night until the age of five.

On average, statistics show that it's only around 66% of children who achieve night-time control at less than three years of age. Under the age of four, around 75% do. Under five years old, it's around 80%, and under six, it's 85%. And bedwetting may continue to be a problem for as many as 10%–13% of six-year-olds, and 7%–10% of eight-year-olds.

On top of this, if a child has one parent who was a bedwetter, they are 75% likely to wet the bed themselves. If both parents did, it rises to 90%. So if your child is still finding this a bit of a challenge, you are not alone.

Most experts do not class night-time accidents as 'bedwetting' or 'nocturnal enuresis' until after the age of five. Remember that staying dry at night involves a whole set of different developmental abilities and physical processes than day-time dryness.

For a child to stay dry at night, their brain must keep a full bladder from emptying, or their bladder must send a strong enough signal to the brain to wake them up in time to use the toilet. This signalling mechanism sometimes takes a while to mature. If it isn't quite up to the job yet, there is little you or your child can do about it. Your child must also have started to produce increased overnight levels of the hormone vasopressin, which suppresses urine production at night. Again, children start to produce this at different ages. And their bladder has to have grown large enough to contain a lot of urine – which also takes a certain physical maturity.

What is sure is that wetting the bed certainly isn't something your child might do through laziness or spite – it is likely to distress them as much as you – so never punish or blame a child for wet sheets in the morning, however near to your wits' end you might be.

DON'T SET YOURSELF UP FOR FAILURE

With everything in perspective, then, we will tackle night-time control in two parts. This chapter will look at the various methods you can use to approach night-time training, assuming that this is a *natural progression from your daytime training*, that you have had no huge problems so far at night, and that you are simply looking for the next step towards completely nappy-free living.

Remember – don't assume that night-time control will be a problem for you. Lots of children take this on board with aplomb, and the whole thing is accomplished as quickly as daytime training. However, if things don't go quite to plan and your child does not seem to be achieving the control they need at night, the next chapter will look at possible causes and some ways you can help them overcome this.

EARLY DAYS

You might, if you are following an Early Days approach to potty training, wonder how on earth it is possible to do without night-time nappies when your baby is still very young. After all, babies wee around the clock. It is only when they are between 18 months and two years old that their bladders become more stable and wait until they are full before emptying, so that they can go longer periods between wees. In the very early days, babies wee every 20 minutes or so! Does this mean no sleep for Mum and Dad for over a year, then?

Since achieving night-time control is not simply a learned skill but is tied up with physiological development, the Early Days approach does indeed involve parent participation 24 hours a day. However, there are degrees of 'participation' – and it's up to you to choose what you, your child and your family are comfortable with.

When should I start?

Some brave parents go for nappy-free nights from the off. The only way you can really achieve this is if you co-sleep. The current government advice is that your child should be in the same room – but not the same bed – as you for the first six months. If you do choose to co-sleep, though, there are many safety rules you can follow to reduce the risk of SIDS (sudden infant death syndrome). Never sleep with your child if you smoke, have been drinking, take drugs or are on medications which cause drowsiness. Put your baby to sleep on their back, don't use pillows or thick covers, and remove any cords, strings or ribbons from your nightclothes or the surrounding area. For more advice on safe co-sleeping, see *The Baby Sleep Bible* (White Ladder, 2009).

Getting rid of nappies at night for very young babies involves being able to detect your baby's cues – a certain squirm, or noise, or cry – which is pretty difficult if they are in a cot away from you, or in another room.

The idea is that, when you detect that your baby has to 'go', you simply sit up and hold them over a potty or large bowl that you keep next to the bed. Many Early Days parents manage this without even turning the light on – the idea is that maintaining darkness keeps melatonin levels high, and helps parents and baby to rest well and feel happy.

Others make the epic voyage to the bathroom at night, and hold them over the toilet or even the bathtub (fewer problems with aim!). Very tiny babies might even manage to 'go' directly onto an open nappy.

If the thought of this gives you the frights, however, you can still maintain your Early Days approach with a less intensive form of night-time training. Some parents opt to put a nappy on their baby in the early days, until the stage when a child would be starting to do night-time training anyway.

Some simply leave the nappy on, and let their baby use it as required. Some put the nappy on as a kind of insurance, but still look out for cues, and offer to take it off and hold them over their pot if they have time.

How to get it right

If your baby is co-sleeping with you, you will want to ensure that your bed stays dry at night – for your sake, your partner's sake, and for your baby's sake. Use a good mattress protector under your sheet, and also a disposable absorbent bed pad. The disposable one can be whipped away and replaced quickly if your baby has an accident, without having to change the whole bed. You can also buy fleecy or lambskin 'puddle pads' for the same purpose, but these obviously need cleaning every time they are weed upon.

You might also put a separate small, *thin*, possibly cellular blanket over your baby which will protect your duvet or covers from accidents – especially 'high' ones from baby boys! But be very careful not to overload your baby with covers, because overheating is a cause of SIDS.

Also, if your baby is nappy free, you will probably want to keep their bottom bare in preparation for speedy danglings over the pot. In order to prevent them from getting cold, then, put them in a cosy top and baby socks, and tuck their legs under the covers. Your own body heat will also keep them warm.

What about naps?

Naptime can work in much the same way as bedtime does. However, if your baby naps in a Moses basket or cot without you beside them, you might need to go down the nappy route until they are consistently waking up dry.

Also, get used to using your baby's cues to encourage them to wee as soon as they wake up from their nap – this can help them get used to the procedure they will need when they learn to do it independently.

> **"** It's not as scary as it must seem, honest! We went for no nappies at night for Lola from about six months. Actually, she doesn't 'go' that often now. When she does need to go, she squirms and digs her feet into my stomach – that usually wakes me up enough to help her go. She uses an old washing up bowl next to the bed with a disposable bed mat under it to catch drips, but we're just starting to take her to the bathroom to do it in the loo. We do it almost in our sleep now … it never takes very long to get back off to sleep again afterwards.
>
> Jane, mother of Lola, one **"**

NON-STOP BOT

When should I start?

There are two schools of thought on this within the Non-Stop Botters' brigade. On the one hand, most experts seem to agree that the majority of children are not ready for night-time training until some time after they have achieved day-time control – usually around 10 months later. The idea would be to conquer the day-time, then wait a few months – possibly until after the age of three – until the child is consistently producing dry nappies in the mornings, and then tackle night-times – with the same intensive, all-or-nothing approach that was used initially.

On the other hand, some Non-Stop Botters ask why they should make the child (and the rest of the family) go through the whole thing twice. Instead, they pick a time (probably slightly later, to ensure night-time physical readiness) – and go for the whole lot at once. On the day the nappies come off, they stay off – even at night.

The advantage of this is that it does not give the child the message that continuing to wee in a nappy at night is acceptable. It gives a clear, straightforward message that doesn't confuse the child: no more nappies. At all.

The only thing to be wary of with the latter approach is that if you try it too soon, and your child cannot cope with the night-times, you risk making them feel out of their depth and a failure, and you may well have to back-track into nappies. So only try it if you genuinely feel your child is mentally and physiologically ready – spend a couple of weeks observing them closely. Look for dry nappies, wet ones, when they happen, if they wee early in the night or just before they wake up – everything.

You should begin **only** when you are convinced that the time is right.

> 66 Only do day–time and night–time training if a child is older with a mature bladder. Most children are not physiologically ready to be dry at night for 10 months after they achieve day–time dryness. Always look for dry nappies in the mornings and after naps before you start, or you will be setting them up for failure.
>
> June Rogers, continence expert 99

How to get it right

The trick with a fast-track approach to night-time control is getting your child to make the mental leap that the insurance policy of a nappy is no longer available to them. You also need to set them up for success – so prepare the bathroom, their bedroom, their clothes and their 'route' as well you can.

Remember, if your child is not physiologically ready, no amount of incentives will magically *make* them dry at night. But if they are having dry nappies, and waking *before* weeing in the bed, the following will motivate them to reach the bathroom:

- Buy your child some appealing 'Big Girl Knickers' or 'Big Boy Pants' – if you can, take them with you to choose them. They will feel excited about wearing them, and it will make the new night-time routine a positive and fun one.

- Always take your child to the toilet just before bed, so that their bladder at least starts off empty.

- Don't allow fizzy drinks from late afternoon onwards. Some parents limit all drinks from an hour before bedtime, although studies seem to show that this makes little difference – it's the bladder-brain signal that needs to work, and this is not connected to the amount of liquid consumed.

- Provide a night-light in their room and possibly on the landing, so that your child's trip to the toilet is not scary and so that they don't trip. Some nervous children would postpone a toilet trip due to fear of leaving their bed.

- Use a waterproof mattress protector, and then absorbent bed pads under the main sheet. These can be changed quickly should a night-time accident occur. Some parents prefer these to using pull-ups, because they don't give the message that nappies are still ok.

- Be positive. If your child is physiologically ready, they may well achieve control in a very short time, especially if they found the Non-Stop Bot approach achievable in the daytime. But don't be disappointed or angry with your speedy child if they are not quite so quick off the mark at night – remember, this is probably a physical thing that is beyond their control.

What about naps?

With nap times, you simply continue the same all-or-nothing approach as with the night-time. Once the nappies are gone, they are gone. Use bed pads, make sure they visit the loo before they sleep, and keep up the praise. There's nothing very complicated about the Non-Stop Bot approach – it just takes some guts, that's all!

> With Lucas, we thought we'd just go for the 'in at the deep end' approach and tried doing day-times and night-times all at once. But he just wasn't ready. He could do the days, but he couldn't do the nights – he was about two years and eight months – and the fact that he was always wet in the mornings started to make him lose his confidence about the days. So we just bought some new pull-ups he hadn't used before and said they were his 'night-time pants' for now, and that took the pressure off. When he'd really cracked day-times, about six months later, we tried again and this time he only had a few odd night-time accidents before he was dry at night. With Edmund, we'll know to wait this time.
>
> Jen, mother of Lucas, four, and Edmund, two

BY THE CLOCK

When should I start?

By The Clock families tend to follow a similar approach to the Non-Stop Botters – just a little less 'gung-ho'. Most By The Clockers wait until their child has fully achieved daytime control, and is waking most of the time with dry nappies. At this stage, they then introduce night-time training in the same gradual, methodical and routine-based way that they did during the day. This is the method currently used successfully in this country by a majority of families.

The idea is that nothing should force, frighten or put pressure on the child – everything is mapped out in easy-to-understand stages, and all requirements on your child are achievable and done with your support and help.

With this approach, some parents use pull-ups for a while, but introduce them as 'night-time knickers/pants' or 'bed pants'. You are making the distinction here between the babyish nappies that they used to use, and the new grown-up night-time pants that they will now use until they are ready for ordinary underwear. If they have already been in pull-ups during the day, buy a different brand so that they make this distinction.

Some parents use this same tactic but instead of pull-ups, use training pants – these look a lot like ordinary underwear but come with a thick absorbent padding and a waterproof lining. Whichever you choose, make sure you only put them on last thing before they go to sleep, and take them off when they wake.

Don't be tempted to use pull-ups or training pants when you're out and about!

When the time comes to buy proper underwear – usually at the stage when your child is dry for, say, at least five mornings a week – make a big deal of it. Take your child shopping. Let them pick whichever hideously garish design takes their fancy! The more they like their pants, the less they will want to make them wet and smelly.

How to get it right

Think about your daytime routine. You have developed this over a long time, and it fits your child perfectly. They are able to deviate from it sometimes when necessary, but generally they know what to expect, what is expected of them, and how to achieve that.

All you are doing at night is extending this same approach:

- From the week before you plan to go nappy-free at night, talk to your child about the big event. Circle the day on the calendar. Buy the pants. Talk through the process – 'Here's the night light so you can see to get to the bathroom, here's where your step will be, and here's the toilet paper, just like in the day, and then you will go back to your room and close the door, and then get into bed and pull up the covers ...'

- Help your child create a 'night-time poster'. Let them draw themselves – or take digital pictures of them – getting out of bed, going into the bathroom, sitting on the toilet, and getting back into bed. It all reinforces the procedure in their brain.

- If your child is nervous, have a 'Night-time Toilet Teddy' or doll who goes to the bathroom with them, sits on the floor and waits for them, and then gets them back to bed.

- Set up a reward system, as you did in the day. Draw a new night-time sticker chart, with moons and stars, and put it on the back of their bedroom door or somewhere prominent. Start to make the rewards relate to bigger accomplishments – three days of dry nights, for example, earns a treat such as a magazine or a trip to the park.

> **❝** With Stanley, the issue was that his bedroom was a little way down a corridor from the bathroom. We put in the usual plug-in night lights and stuff, but we also found a light that is battery powered and is meant to go in your shed or a cupboard – it is a white dome-shaped light which you push, and it comes on for a few minutes before turning itself off. We put that on the wall outside Stanley's door and he loved it – he used to say it was his space man light, and it gave him just enough time to get to the loo and back to bed.
>
> Alex, father of Stanley, five, and Poppy, two **❞**

The other issue is how actively you get involved during the night. In other words – to lift, or not to lift? Lifting is the process of waking your child up in the night and 'lifting' them in a sleepy state to the toilet to do a wee. Some parents do this a couple of hours after their child goes to sleep, or when the adult themselves is preparing to go to bed. Some wake their child every time they themselves wake to go to the toilet.

Advocates of lifting say that it establishes in the child's mind the need to get up in the night for a wee; it reduces the likelihood of accidents; and it helps children whose bladders are still immature to cope with a full 12-hour stretch.

Those who don't advise lifting say that if done too frequently it can disturb a growing child's sleep, and that it doesn't teach a child to recognise their own bodily signals and learn how to go to the toilet at night independently.

If you do go down this route, do not try to lift your child while asleep or very drowsy. Try to:

- Turn the lights on.
- Wake your child and talk to them, telling them where they are going and why.
- Vary the times of lifting a little, so that your child doesn't become conditioned to only 'go' at certain times, rather than when needed.

> **❝** It is important not to lift while the child is asleep, or you reinforce voiding while asleep, which is exactly what you don't want your child to do. We don't generally recommend lifting these days, because emptying the bladder in the night does not encourage the required increase in production of vasopressin, but if you do, wake the child and turn the lights on. **❞**
>
> June Rogers, continence expert

What about naps?

Follow the rule that once your child's nappies are consistently dry on waking from a nap, you can try them without nappies. Some children don't need to go within the period of a short nap, so this might happen quite early on. If it does, you can use this to boost their night-time confidence – 'Look, you are doing so well in your Big Girl Knickers/Big Boy Pants for your naps! You're so clever, I bet you can do it at night-time too soon'.

Remember also to include a toilet visit in your pre-nap routine. Make it as established a part of this routine as a cuddle or a story – again, it will reinforce the procedure for your child.

> **"** We tried lifting Cara. I don't think it worked. She was still often wet in the morning – I think she was weeing just as she woke up. In the end we just stopped doing it. What really seemed to make the difference was switching her bedtime milk drink to tea–time, and also we put a radio alarm clock in her room and asked her to get up and go to the loo when it came on – she seemed to be able to control herself better if she was woken up suddenly than if she woke naturally and was all dozy and slow to get out of bed.
>
> Emma, mother of Cara, eight **"**

GENTLY DOES IT

Parents who follow a Gently Does It approach tend to believe that night-time training should play no part in potty training in general. In fact, many believe that you *cannot actually train* at night - that the abilities needed to remain dry at night are physiological and will happen when they happen, and trying to train before this is futile and possibly damaging.

What you can do, instead, is just encourage good practice - make sure your child is drinking regularly during the day, stops drinking an hour before bed, and is able to reach a toilet easily at night if they want to.

When should I start?

Because of this ethos, Gently Does It parents are very relaxed about night-times. They generally make use of pull-ups – you can still tout them as 'Night-time Pants' to remove the association with day-time nappy use. They watch for dry mornings, they monitor – but they pretty much just wait until their child's biology has kicked in, and triggers them to stay dry all on their own.

Only at this stage do they make a fuss-free transfer from pull-up to proper underwear – after a real physical transition has already been made. No child would choose to wake up soggy and uncomfortable, they reason. Like most developmental milestones, there is a wide range of what is 'normal', and a wide range of acceptable schedules.

❝ We do advise parents that a child should not use pull-ups or pyjama pants after the age of five, when it starts to reinforce the idea in a child's subconscious that they are 'allowed' to use the pull-up rather than the toilet, so it doesn't matter if they do. ❞

June Rogers, continence expert

How to get it right

All you need to do is keep calm and keep an eye out for progress. It is important with an older child that, if they are still not ready to go nappy-free, you don't ladle on the pressure. Because they are older, they will already have an understanding that pull-ups are a bit baby-ish, and that grown-ups sleep in normal underwear. You need to build their confidence and reassure them that you are proud of them, while both of you are waiting for their bodies to catch up.

As with the By The Clock approach, you can use trainer pants and then introduce appealing underwear when you feel the time is right. However, there is less emphasis on sticker charts and rewards, because you are trying to get away from the idea that this is something they have control over – and can therefore be rewarded for.

When you feel that they are ready to go pull-up-free, use bed pads initially, or 'double-make the bed' by layering a sheet, then a pad, then another sheet which can be pulled off if an accident happens, leaving the first sheet dry and ready to go.

If you suspect that using a very efficient pull-up which pulls all wetness away from the bottom is actually delaying things for your child because they don't feel the discomfort, can't tell it has happened, or feel that it's 'ok' to go, then do an 'experiment': let them go bare-bottomed on a bed pad for one night, and see what happens. You might find that their body is ready now, but they just needed a push to set things in motion.

If they make a puddle, don't make a fuss. Just pop the pull-ups back on as usual, and try again in a few weeks.

What about naps?

Naps for Gently Does It children should be as relaxed as night-times. Use pull-ups or training pants, then bed pads when necessary. Your older child might grow out of naps anyway during the time they are getting ready to ditch night-time nappies, so it may not be an issue.

If they still have a nap, though, you could use nap time as the time for your 'experiment' – let them go without a pull-up just for a short nap, build their confidence, and then progress to nights.

> ❝ I waited about three or four months after day-time training before trying it, and if they weren't ready I'd give it another month and keep trying – there's nothing worse than stripping and changing a bed and a screaming upset child at 4am.
>
> Sharon, mother of Callum, six, Vincent, five, and Lauren, four ❞

Girls' Guide

- Many girls love to play with baby dolls and all the paraphernalia that comes with them. Why not let your daughter set up a little crib for her favourite doll next to her own bed, and set up a dolly potty next to it? She can practise getting dolly up to do a wee. You can even introduce a role-play where dolly has an accident, but nobody minds or gets cross, they just clear it up and give her a cuddle and then she tries again.

- Make your little girl's night-time trips to the bathroom as comforting as possible. Girls often wear flimsy nighties and less comforting night clothes than boys, and may feel chilly or exposed when getting out of bed – hang a cosy dressing gown nearby so that she can pull it on before sitting on the toilet.

Boys' Basics

- Many people believe that boys achieve night-time dryness later than girls. Don't worry if he seems to not be ready. Boys are also more competitive, and may well realise that their friends from school are not in pull-ups – try to reassure him that all bodies are different and do things at different times, and that pull-ups are fine for grown-up boys too.

- Boys who wee standing up may be a little precarious on a step if they are sleepy – and falling into the toilet is obviously a drowning risk. Make sure that they have a handle, or towel rail, or something steady to hang on to while they wee, or consider letting them wee into a potty in the bathroom or in their room for a while until they get a little older.

" Achieving night–time dryness is a fine balance between the ability of the bladder to hold on, and the volume of urine produced. If either is not right, the child will slip into bedwetting. Both have to be in place. Until they are, you can still keep a good routine – offer lots of daytime drinks, make sure they go to the loo before bedtime, and ensure they are not constipated. Constipation is actually a fairly common hidden cause linked to bedwetting. **"**

June Rogers, continence expert

Toilet Troubleshooting and Special Situations

 I performed at Mom and Dad's party when I was four. Oh my gosh, I was singing a Madonna song and I peed myself.

Britney Spears, singer

No matter how painstakingly you follow your chosen approach, how calm you remain, how many positive vibes you give out – indeed, how downright perfect your potty training parenting style is – you will probably run into trouble at some point.

It happens to everyone. Even if your child has been completely reliable for several months, things can still go wrong. Sometimes it's a temporary blip; sometimes it feels like a rather unjust slide into chaos after an awful lot of hard work getting it right.

But whatever it is, it is happening to a lot of other parents too. You are not alone. Even if nobody else is talking about it, you can rest assured that if you take a look around your local toddler group or pre-school, a large proportion of the parents there will be dealing with problems the same as, or worse than, yours.

In fact, many of these issues crop up so often that they are common to all *Potty Training Bible* approaches – so in this chapter most of the information will be dealt with by specific 'troubleshooting topic', rather than by approach.

Firstly, let's deal with the most common, if perhaps less serious, parental complaint: 'It's just not working!'

There are quite a few very common reasons children 'fail' at potty training:

- Your child isn't ready – their physical development isn't up to it yet.
- They aren't ready mentally yet – their fears are too great or their desire to do it is too weak.
- Their communication skills aren't good enough to enable them to understand what you want and to tell you what they need.

- They feel an overload of pressure and judgement from their parents.

- You haven't got the time to really devote to seeing your approach through right now.

- You are giving mixed messages as to what you expect from them.

- Your chosen approach doesn't really suit you, your child or your lifestyle, and you need to review it.

- Your child has a physical problem.

You can see that most of the first reasons on the list are developmental ones – and by waiting a few months and trying again, these will probably resolve themselves on their own.

Most of the other reasons are down to you to resolve. Are you really happy with your chosen approach? Do you really have time to do it now? Are you giving your child a fair chance – supporting, not judging? Don't worry if you feel you have been going down the wrong route – just go back to the Introduction, review the options, and see if there is another way which might suit you better.

The last point on the list is the only one with which you might initially need outside help from your health visitor or GP. The most common physical problems will be covered in this chapter.

PHYSICAL PROBLEMS

Constipation

Constipation is the production of dry, hard-to-pass stools. They are often infrequent, but it's the texture that matters – some children 'go' less frequently but are not constipated, because the stool is of normal texture.

Some children get constipated because their diet is quite limited – they don't eat very many fruit and vegetables or whole grains. Constipation can delay potty training because it makes pooing painful and slow, which can lead to fear of pooing, 'holding on', and anal fissures (all covered in more detail below).

The place to start tackling this problem then is in your child's diet. Be sneaky! Mix in whole wheat pasta with their normal pasta – they won't even notice. Be adventurous with fruit – make 'kebabs' by threading chunks onto a blunt skewer, and providing a nice fruity dipping sauce. Bake carrot cake or banana cake – a treat, but with hidden fruit. Make sandwiches with whole bread or, if they won't accept this, make one side with whole bread and the other with white, and serve it white side up. Add blueberries or chopped up prunes to cereal – and then start a game of 'fishing' for the fruit with a spoon. There are some great ideas to get fruit and veg in your child in *5-a-day For Kids Made Easy* (White Ladder, 2010).

And make sure your child has access to enough liquid – offer drinks, keep a lidded cup 'on the go', and never restrict drinks in the daytime.

If you feel that the problem is serious and long-term, your child might benefit from a mild laxative or stool softener, but you should *never* give your child these without seeing a GP first and receiving a prescription for the appropriate medicine.

Anal fissures

An anal fissure is a tiny tear just inside the anus, often caused in children by pushing out a hard stool. You may see some blood on the toilet paper or on the stool. Most fissures heal within a week or two, but the main problem is that some children become fearful of doing a poo because of the pain this causes, and therefore start to retain or 'hold on' to it, making the problem even worse and becoming a vicious cycle.

In order to promote healing as quickly as possible, make sure your child is drinking plenty of fluids and eating fruits and fibre. You can get a special cream from the GP to help the fissure heal and to ease the passage of stools, or you can just use a dab of Vaseline.

> ❝ Ashley had a fissure, and it made life absolute hell for weeks. She just wouldn't do a poo until she absolutely couldn't hold it in anymore, and even then she'd scream and fight us off. She gave herself nasty headaches and stomach aches through holding it in. She'd only 'go' every few days, and as the days built up, she'd be in a worse and worse mood and really grouchy — no wonder! Eventually our doctor prescribed some liquid laxative which eased it, and eventually it went away, but it took ages before she was really normal about going to the loo again.
>
> Tom, father of Rebecca, nine, Ashley, six, and Vincent, three ❞

Diarrhoea

Diarrhoea – runny or watery stools – is often accompanied by vomiting. Because the combination can often lead to dehydration, it is vital to offer water and rehydration salts (there are ones specifically for children available from the pharmacy).

Diarrhoea can be caused by bacteria, a virus, a reaction to a new food, a reaction to antibiotics, or even, if persistent, an allergy to a food. If it carries on for more than a day or two, call your GP – most are more than happy to see your child to check for other physical problems.

The odd thing is that, despite not being 'difficult' to pass, diarrhoea can also sometimes cause anal fissures and irritate the soft membranes of the anus. Keep your child's bottom as clean as you can with wet wipes, and bath them often.

Urinary tract infections

Urinary tract infections (UTIs) can occur in both girls and boys, but are much more common in girls because the tiny tube leading to the bladder is much shorter and the opening is nearer the anus, so bacteria can be easily transferred.

Symptoms include pain on weeing, weeing often but not fully emptying the bladder; a constant dribble of wee in the pants; cloudy or strong-smelling wee; tummy or lower back pain; and sometimes a strong, urgent need to go 'right now'.

If you think your child has a UTI, see your GP who will test the urine and possibly prescribe antibiotics. Some think that UTIs are a cause of day-time wetting, but this is not proven – it is just as likely that the UTI is a result of the wetting, and some studies have shown that even when a UTI is treated, the wetting continues. However, you may well be advised to test your child for a UTI if you have declared that they have a problem with wetting.

You can reduce the likelihood of your child getting a UTI by:

- Making sure your daughter knows how to wipe herself from front to back after a poo

- Helping your son to keep his foreskin clean if he is uncircumcised

- Changing wet nappies, training pants or pull-ups as soon as possible

- Avoiding strong bubble baths and soaps, which can irritate

> " Kitty had a little stage where she was complaining that her wee hurt her. We thought it was a UTI and the doctor took a sample, but it came back negative. Then I changed her bubble bath from a children's fruity one back to a very mild baby one, and the problem went away.
>
> Mary-anne, mother of Kitty, three, and Finn, 11 months "

Tight foreskin

Sometimes boys can develop an infection under the foreskin, which is called balanitis. Often careful attention to hygiene – teaching your son to gently pull back the foreskin as far as it will go and wash and dry underneath it – is enough to get rid of it, and certainly enough to prevent it. More serious cases may need a short course of antibiotics. Symptoms are redness at the end of the penis and pain on weeing – see your GP if these occur. Very tight or painful foreskin should also be assessed by your GP.

Physical abnormalities

These are very rare – but worth knowing about, just in case. Severe intestinal and urinary tract defects are usually picked up at birth, in the first few weeks of life, or at least during the first year.

Hirschsprung's disease is a very rare congenital abnormality which can sometimes show up as very bad constipation. It involves a defect in the nerve supply to the bowel, which prevents the intestine contracting normally to push the faeces downwards, leading to a blockage in the intestinal tract.

Hypospadias is a condition in boys where the urethra is misplaced. Instead of the urethra opening at the tip of the penis, it opens on the underside instead, which means producing a 'normal' stream of wee is difficult or impossible. In severe cases, surgery can be carried out once the child is three.

Less obvious problems may only be diagnosed once you have picked up on a problem later on.

CONTROL PROBLEMS

Day wetting

Children have accidents. Even the most reliable of children can have an off-day, or will wet themselves when upset or very distracted. This isn't what is meant by 'day wetting'.

Day wetting is when a child over the age of five who has been seemingly successfully potty trained, regularly has 'accidents'

– ranging from wet underwear, to fully emptying the bladder down the legs and onto the floor.

When this is consistently happening at pre-school or school, and your child is often sent home in spare uniform and the tell-tale carrier bag of wet clothes, this can be very distressing, both for you and especially for your child.

There are various theories as to why this happens. Some believe it has to do with the child having a smaller-than-average bladder. Some believe it is to do with the signals to their brain demanding more frequent wees. Some think it is about the sphincter and pelvic floor muscles failing to ensure the bladder is completely empty when the child is doing a wee. Some think it is due to psychiatric distress, disturbance or problems at home. Some believe a urinary tract infection can either cause this, or is a symptom of this (due to wetness and bacteria being left close to the opening of the urethra).

Due to the range of suspected causes, there are also a lot of 'treatments' out there – ranging from therapy to drugs which control urination. But most children simply grow out of this problem – only around 1% of healthy children over five still have a problem with day wetting, and even then this is usually only damp pants, rather than a full emptying of the bladder.

So the best thing is to give it a while and monitor the number of wet days per week – you will probably see over time that they become fewer. In the meantime, you can help your child by:

- Encouraging your child to go to the toilet when they *first* feel the urge to wee – and asking them to sit there for a couple of minutes until they are sure all the wee has come out.

- Encouraging them to go often enough – around seven times a day – but don't hound them into going every few minutes, because this will mean their bladder never really gets used to stretching to capacity and emptying fully.

- If they are at school, make sure they are comfortable with the school toilets, and ask their teacher or classroom assistant to keep an eye on them when they visit the toilet.

- Think of a 'secret code' they can use to say to themselves to remind them to go to the loo – such as, 'Break time, wee time!' or, 'Lesson's stopped, check my bot!'

> " Ellie still has accidents at school – not usually whole wees, but lots of damp knickers and wet patches on skirts. We've asked her teacher to help remind her, but it's difficult when they're so busy and there are so many children. It seems to be getting a bit less frequent though – our health visitor said it's common, and not to worry for another year or so, so we're trying not to make a big deal of it – although I do worry that the other children will notice and tease her for it.
>
> Karen, mother of Ellie, six, and Pippa, four "

Nocturnal enuresis (bedwetting)

Some children who wet in the day also struggle with night-time bedwetting. Others are absolutely fine by day and have been for ages, sometimes years, but still have a problem at night.

Bedwetting in an older child is one of the biggest stress factors I have found to affect parents, regardless of their parenting style, potty training approach, background or personality. Unfortunately, it's also a topic not many parents openly discuss with each other – which just makes both children and parents feel even more cut-off, worried and powerless.

So how do you know if your child actually suffers from enuresis?

First of all, enuresis is not the same as having accidents when first going without nappies at night. Bedwetting is wetting the bed over the age of five. If you are following the stages discussed in Chapter Five and have only just embarked on the quest for night-time dryness, don't worry if your child is not reliable yet. As with day-time potty training, learning a new skill takes some adjustment and a few mistakes – it might take a while for your child's developmental abilities to allow them to become totally reliable.

Most experts would only use the term enuresis if your child wets the bed two or more times a week.

Health professionals do not usually recommend that parents seek further help or advice until the child has passed their fifth birthday. Until at least then, any night-time wetting is seen as part of a normal variation in development – some children's bodies mature enough to achieve night-time control early, and others simply need a bit more time.

If, however, your child is five or older and still has a regular problem with bedwetting, you can ask to see your school nurse or be referred to an expert. They will check for urinary tract infections; assess any contributory factors, such as making too much urine overnight, small bladder capacity or constipation; and look for any other possible causes.

At this stage you could be offered a number of treatments that will reflect the findings of the assessment. You could be given a medication for your child to take that will suppress night-time urine production. You will also be advised about simple star chart methods, and the option of an enuresis alarm, which is a thin pad that is put on the bed under your child's bottom (like a bed pad), connected by a wire to an alarm that alerts your child if they begin to 'leak'. The idea is that it eventually teaches your child to wake *before* the wee comes out, and allows them to get to the toilet on time.

Unfortunately, the topic of treatment for bedwetting is a very emotive one. Because there is often a genetic link – parents who once wet the bed are more likely to have children who also wet the bed – many parents remember the negative emotions they themselves went through, and have particularly strong feelings about certain 'treatments', linking them to feelings of shame and humiliation.

Therefore, it is crucial to find a way forward that is right for your child, but which you are also comfortable enough with to be positive about – your child will be particularly sensitive to your own cues and feelings about their 'problem', and will look to you for reassurance and support.

It might help to decide in exactly which ways your child's bedwetting is a problem for you *right now*.

Is it the practical side – wet sheets, wet pyjamas, lots of washing, disturbances in the night and delays in the mornings that bothers you? Is it other people's opinions – disapproving relatives, judgments from other parents, difficulties when your child wants to go on a sleepover? Is it your own feelings about yourself – perhaps a childhood bedwetting issue – and your desire to see your child as 'successful' and 'grown-up'?

Once you have had a good honest look at your own feelings, you can start to put into place some strategies for helping your child and yourself cope with this phase:

- If it's a washing issue, don't feel bad about using 'pyjama pants' and disposable bed pads. Removing a wet pull-up is a lot less traumatic than making a bed at three in the morning.

- If it's other people's opinions, remember that their child probably has other issues their parents don't choose to share with the world – no child is perfect. As for sleepovers, try to arrange one with a sympathetic parent who will help your child discreetly use a pull-up, and help them change it in the morning.

- If it is all about your own feelings, remember how you felt when it was happening to you as a child. You probably felt powerless then. But now, you have the power to help your child to not feel like you did. You can make this different. You *understand* – and so you are in the perfect position to see them through this with as little distress as possible. That's a positive!

Finally, remember that pretty much any child who does not have a serious neurological defect or serious learning difficulties will stop wetting the bed sooner or later – the huge majority by the age of 10. It's a waiting game – but you can make the waiting a little bit easier if you keep things in perspective and remove the pressure.

   ❝ My husband wet the bed until he was 10 or so, and so we were braced for it to maybe be a problem for our children. And true enough, neither of the twins are dry at night. But we're not stressing about it. They wear pull-ups. I'm sure that, given another year or so, they'll grow out of it. My husband has memories of being forced to use one of those bed alarms, and refuses to make them go through it too – and I agree. What's worse – wearing a pull-up or making an eight-year-old feel ashamed and 'defective' for something they can't help?

Jenny, mother of Luke and Perry, both seven **"**

Faecal incontinence/soiling

If you think bedwetting is something of an 'unspoken' problem, wait until you come up against soiling or faecal incontinence.

This can range from constant brown stains on the underpants, to full-on leakage. Quite often this is caused by chronic (long-term) constipation. The stool becomes hard and 'lodged' in the bowel, and runny poo seeps past it and comes out with the child being unaware of it.

If it carries on over a long period, this can even cause the child to lose some nerve sensation in the area, which prevents them feeling when they need to poo, and makes the problem even worse.

What is important to remember is that proper soiling – as opposed to the odd poorly-wiped bottom – is not a problem in itself, but a sign that something else is happening: usually constipation. Follow the tips for reducing the likelihood of constipation, and if it continues, get your GP to check it out.

POWER STRUGGLES AND FEARS

Regression

Just when you thought you had it cracked... your child takes a giant step backwards. This can be the most disheartening of things. It could take the form of:

- A child who is reliably using the potty or toilet by day suddenly having a lot of accidents

- A child who has been dry at night for months suddenly wetting the bed three nights in a row

- A child who has been potty trained for a couple of years failing to control themselves at pre-school or school

- A child who is potty trained appearing to do a wee or poo in their pants or on the floor on purpose

You have to remember that whatever form it takes, it is *temporary*. It's a blip. It doesn't mean that they've failed, or you've failed, or you have to start the whole thing over again. It just means that you have to do a little bit of detective work to find out what might have triggered it, have a little bit of patience, and instigate a low-key 'reminder' plan to get things back on track.

Causes of regression might include:

- A change in routine or location – starting pre-school, for instance

- A big family upheaval – divorce, bereavement, moving house or parental stress at work

- A smaller change in circumstances – a holiday, house guests

- A new arrival – this is a classic: new baby equals less attention for existing child, which equals attention seeking, which equals manipulation of toilet habits and 'babyfication'

- A sudden loss of confidence following a string of accidents, or a public accident such as wetting themselves at school

All you need to do is go back to your chosen Potty Training Approach. Remind yourself of the strategies that worked for you. Go back one step further than the one they have regressed from – that is, if they are fine by day but suddenly wetting the bed at night, keep the daytime routine as usual, but go back to a bed pad and bedtime reminders at night. If they suddenly refuse to do poos in the big toilet, let them use a potty - but have it in the bathroom, and slowly move them back onto the big toilet with an insert, with you holding on to them and with lots of distractions.

It's like riding a bike - a child never really 'forgets' how to do it once they've been through potty training once. They just sometimes have wobbles. With a bit of calm reassurance, they'll soon be back on track.

> **❝** We had a problem with regression with Rebecca when Ashley was born. She was three, and had been dry in the day for six months. But when her little sister came along, she started wetting herself a lot, and asking her Mum if she could have a nappy back on. She also went back to speaking in baby talk. But Tania started getting her more involved in helping out with the baby and being the 'grown-up big sister' and 'Mummy's big girl' and eventually it went back to normal.
>
> Tom, father of Rebecca, nine, Ashley, six, and Vincent, three **❞**

Refusal to do poos/holding it in

A lot of children have a temporary problem with the idea of doing a poo. It can range from only wanting to poo into a nappy and not into a potty or toilet to not wanting to poo at all – to the point where they are causing themselves real pain and discomfort by holding it in at all costs.

Some behaviourists believe that a reluctance to do a poo has something to do with a child not wanting to 'lose' a part of themselves: to let it 'fall off' their body into thin air and then see it flushed away as if it were of no value.

Often, it can simply be the case that the child has been constipated or has an anal fissure which has made doing a poo painful, which then makes the child fearful of doing another one – rather logical, if you think about it.

Some children actually twist their legs into knots and physically refuse to let out a poo when they need one, becoming quite hysterical when it gets to the point that it comes out anyway. This is not at all uncommon.

Things you can do to ease their fears and make pooing less painful are:

- Let your child do a poo onto an open nappy laid in a potty, if they refuse to poo without one. Then gradually work on removing the nappy entirely.

- For a child with an anal fissure, apply a dab of Vaseline before they visit the toilet, to make passing the stool less painful.

- Take your child to the loo 10 to 30 minutes after a meal, which is when they are most likely to poo.

- Don't force them to do a poo, or push, or strain – this can make things even worse by causing fissures. Equally, don't make them hold it in – if you are out in public, for example – because this can cause constipation and other bowel problems.

- Make their pooing environment as relaxing as possible – read stories, play soft music.

- If they want to go but can't, let them lean against you while you rub their lower back in circles and talk or sing to them.

66 We tried putting the nappy in the bottom of the potty so they are almost pooing in the nappy, and also sitting down next to them and talking to them. It doesn't work straight away, but you can praise them for just sitting there, and eventually something will come out and you can reward them with a sweet or sticker, even if it's just a little bit of poo.

Emma, mother of Aisha, seven, Anisa, four, and Omar, two 99

TOILET NO-NOS

Playing with poo

We're not just talking a surreptitious hand down the back of the nappy here. We are talking full-scale, take the nappy off or poo on the floor and then paint with it/use it as putty/transport it in your favourite bucket or truck 'playing'.

This is too much for most parents to handle. It is enough to send even the least squeamish parents running up the street in horror. But again – it's a temporary blip, albeit a grim one. And it is seen as *normal* behaviour.

Imagine – you have spent the first few months or years of your life with your bottom regions constantly covered up with a nappy and held firmly in place. You are aware of *something* going on down there, but this is the first time you have actually seen the product before it is whisked away by an adult bearing a wet wipe. It is only natural that you should be intrigued by what you have produced, and curious as to what you can do with it!

Remember – this is not a 'dirty protest' or naughtiness, it is a sign of an inquisitive child. However, it is not easy for an adult to conceal their disgust. Try, though. What you are aiming for is a calm chat about hygiene and germs and putting poos in the proper place. If you show revulsion, you are likely to instil a sense in your child that their poos are disgusting, and may even trigger them to start withholding poos and become constipated.

Apparently, mothers find their own children's poos less revolting than other children's poos – at least Mother Nature has given you some small tool with which to deal with this!

66 Lucas did this – once! I went into his room first thing in the morning and he'd taken off his nappy, tried to wipe himself with his duvet, and carefully wrapped up the poo in his pyjama shorts. I couldn't be too angry because he'd actually been trying to do the right thing, but we had a

talk about toilets and about waiting for Mummy, and he never did it again!

Jen, mother of Lucas, four, and Edmund, two

99

Handling penises

With little boys, poos are not the only thing to be miraculously revealed once the nappy is removed! This is the first time most little boys really discover their penis – and what a fascinating body part it is.

Sometimes boys fiddle with their willy while sitting on the potty or toilet through sheer boredom or in an absent-minded fashion. Girls sometimes 'go exploring' too. Sometimes boys are fascinated by the change of shape and texture that a willy is capable of, and try to make it happen again. Other boys are actually frightened if they get an erection, because it feels strange and they don't know what's happening.

The first thing to do, with both girls and boys, is check that their genitals are healthy and that they are not touching themselves because they have an irritation or pain.

After that, you can gently tell them that we don't touch our bottom half in front of other people. Distract them by giving them a toy to hold, or a book. And for goodness sake don't go overboard in your reaction, or give punishment – at this age, your child is not seeking sexual stimulation, but is just getting to know their body. Fascination with willies and bottoms is usually short lived and will go away on its own – as long as you don't make a huge issue of it.

Toilet humour

Sometimes the fascination isn't with body parts, but with toilet-related words. You might suddenly find that your child's vocabulary is enriched with all manner of words you wish they wouldn't use, and that they invent a stream of poo-related jokes that are not appropriate in front of your starchy relatives or in the local coffee shop.

Again, making a huge fuss just increases the reaction they are getting and is likely to prolong the problem. If they say something you find offensive, calmly remark that, 'That's not polite and we don't talk like that in our family' and then move on. They will still do it sometimes, especially when they get to school – but at least you can begin to teach them what is socially appropriate.

> " Isn't it funny that the phrase 'bum-bum-poo-poo-wee-wee' can elicit such an enormous amount of hilarity from a six-year-old? Actually, it makes me and Matt laugh most of the time, but we try to hide it because I have visions of Ellie announcing it to the school in assembly or something. She did once tell a friend of mine that her shoes were a poo-poo colour – luckily the friend was not easily offended!
>
> Karen, mother of Ellie, six, and Pippa, four "

SPECIAL SITUATIONS

Special needs/disabilities

There is much advice available to parents of children with disabilities, or special needs. This is just a brief comment on a specialist topic.

It is vital to treat every child as an individual, who must be supported in achieving their own potential and living as independently as possible. They may have a physical disability or a mental one; it doesn't matter – they are still entitled to professional guidance and support, and can apply to the Local Education Authority for a statement of special educational needs, which may include help with toilet training. The help on offer varies from area to area.

Many children with learning difficulties or special needs can follow a usual toilet training plan, and many manage control within a 'normal' timeframe. For those with more serious needs, there are specific programmes available that parents and children can follow – these usually require a high level of parental involvement, at least in the initial stages.

What is certain, though, is that no matter what needs or difficulties your child has, if you work at their pace you can help them achieve some degree of toileting ability. For further advice, see the Further Information section and contact details for PromoCon and Mencap.

Twins and multiples

With twins and multiples, the processes you can use for potty training are the same as for 'singletons'. You can still follow any of the approaches in *The Potty Training Bible*.

The main issue isn't with the method, but with the timing – what do you do if one twin is ready to start potty training, and the other is reluctant or simply not physiologically ready?

There is also often a pressure on parents of multiples to start earlier than they might normally consider, in order to reduce the heavy workload of changing constant nappies.

However, on the plus side, if one of your twins gets the hang of it early on, it is quite likely that they will encourage and help their sibling to do it too – twins compare themselves to each other and follow each other's example. This is especially true if you are using star charts or rewards – no twin will want to be left out!

One good tip for parents of twins who are at different stages of potty training is not to go too overboard on praise for the more advanced twin. Be pleased, by all means, and offer praise, but keep it low key – otherwise you risk your other twin feeling less valued and less able. Competition will be an inevitable part of your children's relationship with each other – there's no need to exacerbate it with comments like, 'Look, your sister's doing it, why can't you do it too?'

Lastly, don't rely on one potty being enough. Avoid squabbles, timing clashes and other disasters by buying at least two, but buy them in the same colour so that you don't get situations where the nearest available potty belongs to the 'wrong' twin.

66 Luke was dry in the day about three months before Perry. We tried really hard not to compare them, and not to force Perry to keep up. In the end, though, what did it was Luke starting to use the big toilet – Perry thought that was cool, and wanted to use the steps, so it spurred him on.

Jenny, mother of Luke and Perry, seven **99**

Coordinating training between two homes

If you and your partner have separated and your child splits their time between two homes, it is essential to come up with a common 'action plan' for potty training: otherwise you risk sending such mixed messages that your child will not progress.

Duplicate everything – potty, books, star charts – and try to reach an agreement at least on the basics, such as when or if pull-ups are allowed, or whether the child uses a potty or big toilet. Also, try to pick an approach together. If this isn't possible, then whoever is making the decision could at least photocopy some details of the chosen approach, or make their chosen reading material available.

Remember, too, to agree on treats – or you might find out that the reason your child is so much more successful at making it to the potty at the other house is because they are being offered chocolate rewards there, while you are only offering stickers!

WHEN TO CALL THE DOCTOR

There are a few things to look out for in the wee, poo and bottom department that require a trip to the GP. Most of the time these things will not turn out to be serious, but always ask for advice if you are in doubt – no doctor will resent checking out a small child.

Call if:

- Your child is passing blood in their wee or poo
- They haven't done a poo for more than four days
- They aren't weeing at least every two or three hours
- Their wee has a strong, unpleasant smell
- They need to wee but can't make it come out
- Their stomach is hard or swollen
- They are drinking and weeing excessively – this can be a sign of diabetes
- You feel out-of-control when they get it wrong and cannot control your anger – this can be a very stressful time, and sometimes the adults need some support and help too

Hopefully this chapter will have given you a run-down of the most common problems, with some tips on how to tackle them. Of course, different problems will crop up at different stages according to which Potty Training Approach you are following.

It is worth reminding yourself that your chosen approach will require different understanding and support from *you* to make it successful:

EARLY DAYS

You have chosen an approach that is suitable for an infant or very young child – so don't forget that this will require a lot of parental involvement. Your child is still very reliant on you – if you feel you cannot give them the time or commitment they need, it would be better to wait and use a different approach, rather than forcing them to take strides they are not ready for. On the other hand, if you do use this approach, you will probably find the bond between you strengthens, and stays with you for life.

When your child gets a little older and needs to make the transition to going to the toilet with other carers or by themselves, they may need more support and encouragement than a child who has learned at a later stage. Don't assume that just because they have been 'so clever' so early on, they won't need your help later.

> " Kitty had a nasty virus a few months ago, and it really made her sleep badly at night. It also meant that she was hot and bothered, and needed more space, so Nigel slept in the spare room to give us more room in the bed, and I used a pull-up for two nights while she got better. It wasn't fair to expect her to deal with night-time toileting. And it made no long-term difference – we were back to normal by the following week.
>
> Mary-anne, mother of Kitty, three, and Finn, 11 months "

NON-STOP BOT

If you and your child are Non-Stop Botters, your child may be at increased risk of feeling the pressures of time and speed. Let them know that, even if it doesn't work out as expected, you are still proud of their progress and there will be plenty of time to fine-tune it.

Don't feel too frustrated if you have bad days. They are learning new skills at a very fast rate – even if they have got the hang of it early on, they will still need time. Practice makes perfect.

> ❝ Josh got chicken pox when he was about two–and–a–half, with lots of spots in his genital area, so nappies were out of the question. We used pants as a cooler option – and before we knew it, he'd potty–trained himself!
>
> Julie, mother of Emma, eight, and Josh, four ❞

BY THE CLOCK

By The Clock children do magnificently within a routine and stun other parents with their ability to cope independently. However, they may often need extra help if they are suddenly required to cope with an unexpected event, or a change in routine or location.

Be patient with your child. Help them feel reassured by keeping as many things consistent with their usual routine as possible. Books, teddies and usual potties or toilet inserts all help. They will do you proud – just give them time to adjust and keep up.

❝ Poppy has recently started at a playgroup, and we had a few accidents in the first two months or so. Funnily enough, she was fine in the day at the playgroup, but started wetting herself afterwards at home. The playgroup leader said it was probably due to extra tiredness, and to being a bit unsettled. We started bringing her straight home for a snack and a rest after playgroup, rather than going into town or doing jobs, and it seems to have done the trick – she's dry again.

Alex, father of Stanley, five, and Poppy, two **❞**

GENTLY DOES IT

Your Gently Does It child will probably amaze you with how quickly they become independent once you – or they – instigate training. But one issue that can arise is that, in the meantime, they may feel babyish or may be teased by their peers for still wearing nappies or pull-ups.

Tell them that it is because you know they are so clever and so grown-up that you have decided to let them make the change to toilets when *they* want to, rather than making them do it like a little baby. Reassure them that because they are older, they will be able to make a better job of it. Boost their confidence.

Also, make sure that your child isn't still in nappies just because they – and perhaps you – have simply got used to it. They might actually be ready, but either too lazy to make the change or waiting for a cue to do it. Suggest gently that they might like to try... and let them make a plan with you on a calendar when they will start.

> 66 Don't start potty training just before they go to pre-school – it puts so much pressure on you and on the child, and then they have to keep it up just when they are going through an enormous disruption and change in routine. If you're going to do it, do it a good while before they are due to start. Using the loo needs to be completely normal to them before they have to do it away from home.
>
> Emma, mother of Cara, eight. 99

Girls' Guide

- To help prevent infections, buy cotton knickers. When washing, use a gentle detergent and rinse thoroughly.
- Don't use talcum powder with girls – it can cause vaginal irritation.

Boys' Basics

- If your son wants to stand up to wee but can't aim into the potty or is too small to use the toilet, you can buy a small 'urinal' style plastic toilet for boys – one model even flushes. They are great for preparing boys for pre-schools or schools with urinals.

- Sometimes irritation of the foreskin or penis can be caused by swimming in chlorine-treated pools, or using strong biological laundry detergents. Try swapping to a gentler detergent for the children's washes, and always help your son shower carefully after a swim.

> **❝** I would advise parents not to leave their children in nappies beyond the age of about three-and-a-half. Once they start nursery, this causes so many problems for the child. The child needs to understand that a pull-up is not a long-term solution. Many of the cases we see are children who have become used to the fact that their pull-up is a kind of portable toilet. Who would want to stop playing, go into a different room, get undressed, go to the toilet, wash hands and then come back having missed their turn in the game or the end of the television programme, when they can just do it on the spot? They have to be gently encouraged along the way not to see nappies or pull-ups as an option. **❞**
>
> June Rogers, continence expert

What to Buy
– Equipment,
Books and
Incentives

❝ You can't pee like a puppy, if you are going to run with the wolves.

Don Mashak, political activist **❞**

Going into potty training without some potty training gear is like going into battle without your weapons. Certain basic items of equipment have been mentioned throughout the book, but this chapter is intended to give you more detail on the range of products available to you – and which products might be particularly useful in your chosen *Potty Training Bible* approach.

POTTIES

Seems an obvious one – but wait until you see the variety available! Of course, you don't actually *need* any potty at all if you are going straight to the toilet stage – and even if you do opt for a potty, the most basic and inexpensive one will do just fine – but if you are looking for something a little more deluxe, you will find plenty.

The options are:

Basic 'traditional' potties

These are the potties most of us remember from our own childhoods. They are all-in-one designs: plastic, low and simple.

Pros:
- They are inexpensive, which means you can buy several (for upstairs, downstairs, the car, Granny's house) without busting the bank.

- They are small, so they don't require lots of space in small houses or flats.

- They are easy to get on and off, for smaller toddlers.

- You can also buy smaller 'pee pots' for tiny babies – although any small bowl with high sides will do.

Cons:
They can be a little unsteady depending on the design, and can be easily tipped or moved by a child.

Great for **Non-Stop Botters** who won't need potties for long, and for **Early Days** babies who need smaller potties.

Potty chairs

These are potties with a 'commode-style' lift-out bowl or insert, which sits in a large plastic chair or frame.

Pros:
- They are larger and sturdier than traditional potties, which makes them more suitable for an older toddler or child.

- The insert can be easily lifted out and its contents disposed of, which is handier for the parent and often easier to keep clean and hygienic.

- They usually have 'arms' and a back, which gives a sense of security to a child who feels vulnerable or nervous about using a potty.

Cons:
They are more expensive than traditional potties, which may be an issue for parents who feel their child won't be using it for very long.

Great for **Gently Does It** children who need sturdier models.

'Bells and whistles' potties

Where to start? You can buy potties in the shape of animals with the 'potty bit' in the animal's back; you can buy an 'eco-potty', which is made of plant material and can be buried in the garden at the end of its life to biodegrade and feed your flowers; you can buy potties in a high gloss finish which look more like ornaments than potties (for the style conscious); you can buy potties that flush, potties that sing or potties that change colour when a wee or poo is produced; potties with integrated holders for loo roll; you can find potties in the shape of a urinal, for boys who want to stand to wee; potties shaped like proper adult toilets; potties shaped like cars, with wheels; potties that convert to bathroom steps. The potty choice, in short, is extensive. But why would you opt for a deluxe model?

Pros:

- You can tailor your choice of potty to your home circumstances, space available and family ethos.

- You can find a potty which matches your child's individual needs, and reflects their fears and interests.

- You can tempt a reluctant potty trainer by engaging their imagination.

- You can find a product which will make the transition to using the big toilet easier and more attractive.

Cons:

These don't come cheap. Some of them are also rather large. Make sure you are choosing your potty with your child in mind, rather than being taken in by lots of parent-targeted features!

Great for **By The Clock** potty trainers, who might need something to maintain their interest as they follow their routine.

> 66 Pippa absolutely refused to use the potty chair that her big sister Ellie had used. It was only when we went shopping and got a new pink one with a sticker in the bottom that changed colour that everything changed – she immediately loved it and used it pretty much without any accidents from that day on.
>
> Karen, mother of Ellie, six, and Pippa, four 99

TOILET EQUIPMENT

It's all about making the 'big toilet' comfortable, safe and less intimidating. I would recommend at least a basic insert. Imagine trying to do your business perched on the side of the bath, without being able to touch the floor ...

Toilet inserts

These are plastic mini-seats which sit on top of your usual toilet seat, and make the 'hole' smaller. Some come with handles on the sides so that your child has somewhere to hold on. Some have a small support at the back. Some seats are padded for comfort, and some even have a kind of small ladder attached, which leads up to the seat from the front of the toilet. There are many which come in bright colours or with character designs on.

Pros:
- They make the transition from potty to toilet easier and less intimidating.
- They mean that you can omit the potty stage altogether if you choose to.

- They allow your child to sit in the correct position for easy weeing and pooing, and give them a sense of security.

- They can be used on various toilets within your house, or elsewhere.

- They are easier to wipe and disinfect than a grown-up toilet seat, and therefore are safer for your child to hold on to.

Cons:

Make sure you get one that really fits your toilet seat. An insert that slides, moves or pinches will put your child off the toilet. Some models come with an adjustable bit underneath so they can be properly and snugly fitted.

Great for **Non-Stop Botters** going straight to the toilet option.

Toilet seats

These are similar in purpose but instead of being a separate insert, come as part of an adult toilet seat. The smaller, child-sized seat fits inside the toilet lid, and is hinged in the same way as the adult seat. When the child needs to use the toilet, you simply unclip their seat from the lid and lower it down onto the larger seat.

Pros:

- They are discreet and, when folded up into the lid, cannot even be seen when the lid is down.

- They are handy for bathrooms or downstairs loos with little space, as they don't clutter the room up with 'baby gear'.

- They promote the sense that the child really is using the adult toilet and is 'grown-up'.

Cons:

They require you to replace your usual toilet seat with the new version, which can be pricey. And of course they are not portable, so you may need to buy more than one for your home, and quite possibly a plastic insert for use away from home. These are a good option for Granny's house, for instance, where their unobtrusiveness will appeal, but they are not needed every day or required to be flexible.

Great for **Gently Does It** children who want to feel grown up.

> We found that just leaving our plastic toilet insert on the loo all the time, pretty much, helped the children get used to being able to go to the toilet whenever they wanted without us having to prepare everything. If an adult wanted to use the loo, they'd just take it off and then replace it afterwards.

Tom, father of Rebecca, nine, Ashley, five, and Vincent, three

OTHER BATHROOM GEAR

We've already talked about making a bathroom child-friendly: the best way is to get down on your knees and try to see – and reach – everything from their level. But steps in particular make the business of using the toilet and the sink much easier – and they can be recycled into 'kitchen steps' for budding young cooks when they're no longer needed in the bathroom.

Steps

I think a set of steps in a bathroom is a 'must buy'. These come in various forms and are made of either wood or plastic. The plastic ones are usually in the form of a simple hollow 'box' and are inexpensive. The wooden ones look nicer and last longer, but are pricier. Some have two steps, and incorporate a little storage area under the bottom step for wipes or books. Some have a bottom step which pulls out, giving a larger standing area and less of a steep climb.

Pros:

- They make the bathroom useable and promote the independence of your child.

- They make the big adult toilet useable and less intimidating.

- They encourage your child to wash their hands properly at the big sink, and also to clean their teeth.

- They can be used elsewhere in the house too, with supervision.

- They allow your child to sit in the correct position on the toilet, to plant their feet firmly on a hard surface, and to push when then they need a poo.

- They give reassurance and help your child's confidence on the toilet.

Cons:

They can also give your child access to other areas in your bathroom that you might not have thought about. Can your child use the steps to open a bathroom cabinet, or reach cleaning products, or a window? Make sure you thoroughly child-proof your bathroom with this added height advantage in mind. And look for steps with a slip-proof tread – some wooden ones can become slippery if a child drips water from the tap, or is wearing socks.

Great for **By The Clock** children learning bathroom routine.

> ❝ Get some steps – ours are wooden ones and have lasted for ages. They're now used downstairs in the kitchen and sometimes out in the garage when we're doing some woodwork.
>
> Matt, father of Luke and Perry, seven ❞

Moist wipes

These are available in pharmacies and supermarkets, and look like wet wipes but are marketed at the 'bottom wiping' end of the market! There are some well-known brands, but the supermarket own-brands work very well and are less expensive. Some come with a colourful plastic box to store them in, which you can place on the cistern or near the toilet.

Some wipes also have a coordinating range of foaming soaps to encourage hand washing.

Pros:
- Their appealing designs make children more inclined to want to learn to wipe their bottom.
- A moist wipe is more effective at cleaning a bottom after a poo than dry toilet paper.
- They can help if a child has a fissure, or generally sore bottom, because they are gentler on the skin.
- They can be flushed down the toilet just like normal paper, so no mess.

Cons:
They are an added expense when used every day, and some parents feel that they are a bit of a marketing con – children

have managed very well without their 'own' version of loo paper until now! Some parents have also expressed concern that they contain mild detergent chemicals which they don't want to apply to their children's skin on a regular basis.

UNDERWEAR

Whether you opt for training pants, pull-ups or proper underwear, it needs to be different enough from their nappy to signal, 'Here we go! This is different, this is clever, this is grown-up – and this is worth keeping clean and dry!' Here are some options:

Training pants

These are fabric pants, usually made from cotton, which have elasticated legs and an absorbent layer, with a plastic waterproof guard. They are designed to look and feel like 'normal' underwear.

Pros:

- They make your child feel grown-up and want to progress from nappies to underwear.

- They give you the security that accidents won't cause catastrophic messes.

- They don't 'lock the moisture away' in the same way that nappies and pull-ups do, which means a child can still feel the wetness, giving them more incentive to reach a toilet before 'going'.

- A child is less likely to become dependent on training pants than on pull-ups.

- They can be washed and are hard-wearing, so they're therefore a less costly and more environmentally friendly alternative to disposables.

Cons:

They need washing. Which might be a bit grim, depending on the accident! Also, some parents feel that you might as well go the whole hog and move straight onto proper underwear. And the plastic layer can be problematic in very warm weather, or if a child has a rash or soreness.

Great for **By The Clock** children who are taking it steadily but surely.

Pull-ups

Pull-ups are a fantastic alternative to a normal nappy, because they are pulled on and worn like 'normal' underwear, and yet can deal with most accidents your child can throw at you. Where they are most useful is when you are doing day-time potty training but don't want to start night-time training yet – you can buy an unfamiliar brand of pull-ups that you can present to your child as 'night-time pants', and therefore make the distinction between being allowed to wear this at night, but not a nappy by day.

Pros:

- Easy and effective

- A psychological step on from nappies

- Can be thrown away rather than washed

Cons:

Using pull-ups for a long period of time is expensive, and some parents don't like the negative environmental impact. Also, an older child may become lazy about toilet training if they wear them for too long, because they take away the discomfort of having an accident.

Great for **Non-Stop Botters** who have mastered daytimes quickly but need reassurance at night for a while.

'Proper' underwear with child-friendly designs

There are a lot of lovely designs of children's underwear out there – and once you are at that stage, it is worth finding some that really appeal to your child, to give them the added incentive of keeping them nice.

Pros:
- They are visually appealing and therefore have a psychological incentive.

- They can be used as a 'reward' for keeping plain pants dry for a certain length of time.

- They will help your child feel grown-up and therefore ready to complete their toilet training successfully.

Cons:
They will give you lots of washing if your child isn't ready for them yet. Set them up for success by making sure they are physically ready before taking them on a shopping trip to buy some. Look for the ones that come in multipacks from baby stores and supermarkets – they are appealing but good value, and can be replaced cheaply if they get badly stained.

Great for **Non-Stop Botters** who are going in at the deep end.

❝ Pants with pictures or designs on are fantastic. You just say, 'You don't want to get Spiderman all wet, do you?' and it gives them that incentive to keep them dry.

Janet, childminder, mother of Sarah, Debbie and David, now grown-up, and grandmother of Jamie, two **❞**

❝ Emma was a text-book child who was easily bribed by choosing her very own grown-up knickers (Tweenie ones in her case). The incentive was that if she went a week without wetting her boring plain practice ones, she could wear the fancy ones.

Julie, mother of Emma, eight, and Josh, four **❞**

TRAVEL GADGETS

Obviously travel gear is all about being portable, flexible and useful. No, these products are not always necessary – we just stuck a normal plastic potty in our car boot, and never owned a foldable travel one – but it does depend on your circumstances and how often and far you travel.

Travel potties

There are various designs available. Some fold up small, and are ideal for putting in a bag or even a large pocket. Some have lids, to prevent spills in the car. Most involve putting a small plastic potty liner inside, which can then be tied up and disposed of in the same way as a nappy sack. Some even convert into a toilet insert, so are great for use as either a potty or on a public toilet while away from home.

Pros:

- They make life more flexible while travelling, especially by car, because they can be used by the side of the road, or in a car park or service station, or even on the back seat or boot of a car.

- They are neat and can be carried around in a bag on a day out.

- They take the stress out of travel, because you don't have to hold on until the next service station or public toilet.

Cons:

If you're only going to be using it in the car, you don't really need one that folds up. They can also be a little flimsy for children who feel vulnerable sitting on a potty. And you need to clean them well and have some antibacterial wipes on hand to prevent smells!

Great for **Early Days** babies who need to wee often while out!

Foldable toilet seats

These perform exactly the same function as ordinary plastic toilet inserts, but they are made so that they fold into four small sections, which can be easily carried in a bag.

Pros:

- They mean you don't have to wander around with an obvious loo seat under your arm!

- They provide reassurance and protection in public toilets and in unfamiliar loos on holiday.

Cons:

Some designs are so thin and hard in order that they fold up small, that they sacrifice comfort for delicate bottoms. Look for the designs that are soft and slightly padded, but still fold away. If your child is bigger and doesn't need the support, but you are concerned about hygiene in public toilets, you can buy disposable toilet covers that are made of paper and cover the seat. You can also get disposable mittens to cover your child's hands, if they like to hang onto the seat.

Great for **Gently Does It** children going straight from nappy to toilet who need extra support.

Car seat protectors

These are fitted waterproof covers which sit snugly on a child car seat and prevent any accidents from seeping through to the seat below. They buckle in and don't affect the safety of the seat.

Pros:

- They prevent your child's car seat from smelling and protect it from dampness.

- They are safe to use with the seat, and won't compromise its safety features.

- They can also be used in most buggies, so you get good value for money.

Cons:

Make sure you fit it properly, or wee can leak out. Read the instructions and apply them to the letter – don't install anything in your child's car seat that makes it difficult to buckle up, or which reduces the snugness of the straps.

Great for **Early Days** children who are more likely to wee while sleeping deeply on car journeys.

❝ We don't have a car seat protector, but we did use a disposable bed pad folded in half – they're so thin they don't bulk them up or get in the way of the buckles or anything. These days we just put one in if we're coming home late at night or if Mason's likely to fall asleep.

Kerry, mother of Mason, four **❞**

BED PRODUCTS

These are anything that makes the miserable process of night-time bed stripping less traumatic. This will not only help you cope with sleep interruptions, but will also lessen the psychological effects of night-time accidents on your child. Research has shown that a reaction of anger and punishment when a child has wet the bed certainly doesn't improve their behaviour, but usually makes it worse. The key is quick changes and less work.

Disposable bed pads

These are a 'saddle style' disposable mat with ends that tuck under the mattress on either side to keep them in place. They don't cover the whole bed – they just form a wide strip of protection under your child's hip area, covering from their upper back to their knees. They are used under their normal sheet, or can be used in a 'sandwich' between two sheets, so that if the top sheet is weed upon, it can be whipped off and the bottom one is still dry, having been protected by the bed pad.

Pros:

- Even if your child is wearing pull-ups to sleep in, they sometimes leak, and changing a bed pad is much easier and less dramatic than stripping a whole bed.

- For children who really want to try wearing normal underwear at night, a bed pad provides an insurance policy for the parent and reassurance for the child.

- They prevent wee from soaking into mattresses, which is difficult to clean and can smell.

Cons:

If your child is wetting them every night they can start to become expensive. Better for children who just have the occasional accident.

Great for **Gently Does It** children who are training later but don't want to be seen as babyish.

Waterproof mattress covers

These are fitted sheets with a plastic waterproof backing that fit over the whole of the mattress, under your child's normal sheet. They often have a terry towelling or soft cotton upper-side for comfort.

Pros:

- If it's a large puddle, it can't leak over the side of the protected area because the whole bed is protected.

- It can be washed, which is less expensive and perhaps more environmentally-friendly than disposable pads.

- It looks like a normal sheet, and often the child doesn't even notice it or realise what it's there for, which can help if your child feels embarrassed by night-time leaks.

Cons:

Be aware that they are plastic-backed, which can make a child hot and sticky – especially in warm weather – and shouldn't be used if your child has a temperature. Some designs cannot be tumble-dried either, so you will need two for a quick change-around.

Good also for family beds with **Early Days** babies in them – you can buy waterproof mattress covers in double and King size.

66 Use all the modern help available, but don't make a big deal of putting on pyjama pants. Saying, 'You won't need these when you're a big girl' is a sure way to wear down her self-esteem. If you don't have a waterproof mattress protector, an old-fashioned 'draw sheet' is a useful standby. Just fold a sheet in half or thirds and tuck it in crossways under your child's hips. If it gets damp, it's easy just to pull it out without re-making the bed and disturbing sleep.

Annie, author's mother and grandmother of Evie, six, and Charlie, two 99

LIGHTING

Good lighting makes a lot of difference to how willing a child is to visit the loo at night. It needs to be dim enough not to disturb sleep or prevent the child from falling asleep in the first place, but strong enough to light steps and doorways and provide reassurance.

You might like to look at plug-in night lights which give off a soft glow in your child's room or in a corridor or a landing. You could give an older child a light that glows softly as a night light but can be taken off the base and used as a torch for trips to the loo. There are even 'intelligent' lights that work off the main ceiling light, and which respond to your night-time needs – you can programme them to give off a soft light for night-time wakenings or loo trips, and they can be set to softly light stair wells and landings.

Pros:

- The right lighting can persuade a reluctant night-time toilet-goer to brave the world outside their bedroom door.

- They come in appealing designs, many of which can be operated by the child themselves.

Cons:

It is important that a child has a certain level of darkness at night in order to fall asleep properly and for the brain to regenerate. Make sure the light level isn't too high or garish. Soft, low glows are better than anything bright, flashing or highly-coloured. And if you are thinking of using fairy lights or strings of lights, make sure they are approved for use in children's bedrooms – they must be safely wired and cool to touch. Keep wired lights well out of reach, and never use ones intended for garden or Christmas tree use.

> **❝** Marnie had a fish tank in her room which was back-lit and gave off a glow at night, but wasn't too bright. She also loved looking at the fish while she was falling asleep.
>
> Maxine, mother of Marnie, 11, and Freddy, five **❞**

POTTY BOOKS

There are so many fantastic children's books about potty training available now. Many come with their own sticker charts in the back, or with DVDs. Look for ones that are appropriate to your child's age and gender. There are two main options:

Story books

These come as board books or picture books, and are just like normal children's story books, except that the central theme or character is potty training related. They tell a story of a character – they might concentrate on a particular issue such as fear of the big toilet, or bathroom hygiene – and they are usually illustrated with coloured drawings in the manner of a standard child's picture book.

Pros:

- They are appealing and have a familiar look and feel to them.

- They reach out to a child's imagination, and present information to them in a softly, softly manner that doesn't preach at them.

- They often feature animals or toys as main characters, which can be less confrontational than books featuring human boys and girls.

- They are fun!

Cons:

Be careful that the central potty issue is not too obscure. Some mask the issue so heavily with tales of animals and fantastic characters that many young children simply won't pick up on the message. Make sure the storyline is simple and clear.

Information books

These books have more of a 'real life' feel to them. They often feature photographs of real toddlers sitting on their potties, washing their hands and so on. They are less story-based, and instead use simple sentences to describe the actions of the children in the pictures.

Pros:

- Children like to look at pictures of other children.

- Children will see the 'book children' as their peers, and want to emulate them.

- The pictures are clear and informative. They show your child exactly how to do things and what is expected of them, which takes away some of their apprehension.

Cons:

A child who is very reluctant to start potty training may not be willing to share a book like this with you, and may be better off reading a story-based potty book that is less obviously asking them to do something, and will engage their imagination.

Great for **Non-Stop Botters** or those who need to get a good idea of what they need to do *quickly*.

66 We've just bought Sara a potty training book that has pictures of a little girl using a potty and she thinks it's hilarious. She loves it. A friend of mine also suggested that you sit the child down on their potty in front of a low mirror so they can see themselves — we tried this and she was absolutely absorbed. It kept her sitting there far longer than she would have done otherwise.

Gemma, mother of Sara, two, and Phoebe, nine months 99

TOYS/DOLLS

We bought my daughter Evie a doll that weed, and she actually found it faintly disturbing. She was quite alarmed by the hole in its bottom where the 'wee' came out, and after a couple of days of sitting rather pathetically on a dolly potty next to Evie's big one, the poor thing was perfunctorily dressed and banned from potty service entirely.

However, many parents swear by them. Girls especially seem to find them rather fascinating – although how much of the attraction is potty-related and how much is pure dolly enjoyment is a moot point. And of course the dollies come with accessories such as their own little potties, so that children can do role-play with them.

There are also boy baby dolls available, which wee from a proper willy.

Pros:

- They can engage a child in the whole process of weeing in a potty.

- They can help a child to role-play, which may help them play out any concerns or fears they have about potty training or toilet use.

- They can distract a child while they sit on a potty or toilet, which will keep them there longer and help them 'produce' something.

Cons:

How effective these toys are really depends on your child. And the fact that the child has to put water in one end before it comes out the other end can be rather messy for your carpets, and a nuisance for the parent who has to oversee the whole process. Also, avoid those dolls that you actually feed with a special kind of paste, which they then eliminate with glee. Parents have regaled me with tales of explosive results.

> 66 We have friends who have the boy dolly who wees. I found it all a bit too anatomical for my liking! But their kids – they have a boy and a girl – love it. Our boys gave its willy a few yanks and then ignored it.
>
> Jen, mother of Lucas, four, and Edmund, two 99

INCENTIVES

Of course, you can simply dig out an old Tupperware box from the back of the cupboard, fill it with your chosen 'rewards' and leave it at that. But many parents swear by sticker charts, and this is an age where children are especially motivated by rewards and praise. Even if you buy one, find a way to get your children to take ownership of it as much as possible – let them stick it up on the wall, or add to it, or draw on it. And be consistent with it – if you go a couple of days without using it, your child will know it doesn't really matter to you, and will invest less commitment in it too.

Sticker charts

You can, of course, help your child draw their own, but there are some fantastic ones in the shops which feature princesses, knights, dinosaurs, and all manner of character-led illustrations.

You need to decide exactly what your child will get a sticker for. A wee? Every poo? A whole day or night dry? Be consistent, and don't forget to do it – you can bet your child won't!

Pros:
- They help your child 'take ownership' of the process and of their own success.

- They boost self-esteem and reward effort.

- They provide clear, visual evidence of their successes – which can later be shown to Mummy and Daddy, or to grandparents, for example.

- They give your child something to aim for.

Cons:
They can be a bit expensive. If you don't feel like getting out the crayons and creating your own, why not download a free one from the internet? These are a great compromise, because they don't cost a penny, but often have designs which can be coloured in and added to by your child, giving them the chance to really make it their own.

Great for **By The Clock** children and those following a routine, to keep up interest and motivation.

> ❝ We had a book with its own sticker chart in it for Cara, but actually she ended up drawing her own one with her Gran, which she glued all sorts of sparkles and stuff onto, and she was so proud of it that she really wanted to fill it up with stickers. It worked much better than the bought one. ❞
>
> Emma, mother of Cara, eight

GIRLS' STUFF AND BOYS' STUFF

Lots of the above products work well for girls or boys. But there are a couple of things out there which are specifically aimed at a particular gender.

Girls

If your daughter really loves to role-play and surround herself with toys, she might like a mini version to play with. You can buy a book that comes with a miniature dolly and a mini potty. This is good for when your child is actually sitting on the potty or toilet herself, and a larger dolly would be cumbersome or heavy for her to manoeuvre.

Boys

Toilet balls go in the water in your toilet, and the idea is for your son to aim his stream of wee at them. Great for target practice!

You can also get a plastic gadget that clips onto the toilet seat and hangs down the front, which he can wee into like a mini-urinal. It can then be tipped straight into the loo without unclipping. Good for boys who want to stand and wee but aren't tall enough to aim into the toilet yet.

AND FOR THE CHILD WHO HAS EVERYTHING ...?

What about talking toilet paper? Yes, really. You can buy a toilet paper holder onto which you can record your own voice. Got a reluctant handwasher? Why not have your loo roll suggest that, 'It's time to wash your hands'? Or perhaps record an encouraging message: 'Well done Lucy, way to go!'

The business of potty training can be as simple or as laden with gadgets as you choose to make it. Some gadgets are fun, some are pretty much essential, some are modern classics. I hope this gives you an overview of some of the possibilities.

> 66 PromoCon can also help to signpost families who need portable potties, toilet seats, toddler and child swimwear for children who are not yet toilet trained, and washable trainer pants. 99
>
> June Rogers, continence expert (see p181 for details)

A Few Final Words

" Ok that's it, talking poo is where I draw the line.

Eric Cartman (South Park) **"**

It's amazing how some very basic bodily functions can get us talking, crying, tearing our hair out, sharing stories, hiding secrets, and hopefully sometimes even laughing.

This book is for what I call 'real parents'. Not those pretend parents we all try to live up to, who only wear pristine white and beige neutrals; have never consumed a chicken nugget; and live in Catalogue World where floors are always glowingly restored wood, children's bedrooms are bedecked in tasteful hand-sewn bunting rather than jungles of plastic toys; and nobody ever has to fish a pair of wet pants from under their little darling's bed.

I hope that it has helped you to recognise the approach you are looking for on the quest for a nappy-free life. I hope it has laid out the options, and given you some great tips for doing what *you* want, the way *you* want to do it.

But most of all I hope it has reminded you to trust yourself. Read the book, listen to your friends, ask your parents, ignore that annoying woman at toddler group who never eats the kids' biscuits, but above all – trust yourself.

You know best. You know your child best. It's your life. I hope whichever potty training approach you choose works brilliantly for you – but remember, however many puddles you have to mop up, however many times he misjudges his aim, however often she 'forgets' to go, however often you buy more carpet cleaner ... it doesn't last forever.

One day your small person will be a big person. And will be able to *go to the toilet* at will. With no messes. Well, hardly any (we'll cover how to deal with inebriated teenagers and adult wedding guests at a later date).

Good luck! And don't let the puddles get you down!

Further
Help and
Information

ERIC (Education and Resources for Improving Childhood Continence)

Provides information and support on childhood bedwetting, day-time wetting, constipation and soiling, to children, young people, parents and professionals. It has a website with resources for parents and children.

www.eric.org.uk

0845 370 8008 (Monday–Friday 10am–4pm)

Mencap

Offers a helpline that advises on all aspects of life with learning difficulties and disabilities. It will also put families in touch with other support services.

www.mencap.org.uk

0808 808 1111 (Monday–Friday 10am–6pm, weekends and bank holidays 10am–4pm)

ParentlinePlus

A parent support organisation that offers a confidential helpline where parents can talk to other parents and receive non-judgmental advice and support. It will also direct you to regional support groups.

www.parentlineplus.org.uk

0808 800 2222 (24 hours a day)

PromoCon

Works to improve the life for all people (children and adults, and those with disabilities) with bladder or bowel problems, or continence difficulties. It advises both parents and professionals.

www.promocon.co.uk

0161 834 2001 (Monday–Friday 10am–3pm)

white LADDER

the parenting & family health experts

Get 30% off your next purchase...

We are publishers of a growing **parenting and family health** range of books. We pride ourselves on our friendly and accessible approach whilst providing you with sensible, non-preachy information. This is what makes us **different from other publishers**.

And we are keen to **find out what you think** about our book.

If you love this book **tell us why** and tell your friends. And if you think we could do better, **let us know**. Your thoughts and opinions are important to us and help us produce the best books we possibly can.

As a **thank you** we'll give you 30% off your next purchase. Write to us at **info@whiteladderpress.co.uk** and we'll send you an online voucher by return.

Come and visit us at **www.whiteladderpress.co.uk**

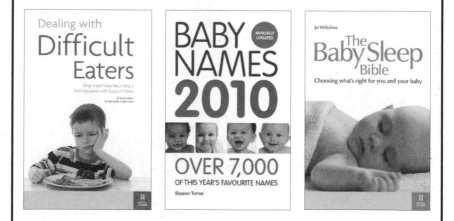